LAUGH MORE

Cover & design by SpiffingCovers Ltd.

www.samrehan.co.uk

Published by
Love of Life Publishing

Paperback ISBN - 978-1-8382817-0-0
.mobi ISBN - 978-1-8382817-2-4
.epub ISBN - 978-1-8382817-1-7

THE 9-STEP LAUGHTER WELLNESS JOURNEY
THAT WILL HELP YOU TO

LAUGH MORE

SOAR IN YOUR HEALTH,
CAREER AND RELATIONSHIPS

SAM REHAN

CONTENTS

About Sam Rehan ..... p 6
Feedback for Sam ..... p 7
Dedications ..... p 11
Disclaimer ..... p 13
Foreword ..... p 14

INTRODUCTION:

How Laughter Helped To Save A Man's Life ..... p 17

PART ONE:

Welcome To Laugh More ..... p 23
Chapter 1: *Why Laugh More?* ..... p 31
Chapter 2: *What Is Laughter And How You Can Make It A Choice* ..... p 41
Chapter 3: *Start Your Laughter With A Smile* ..... p 57
Chapter 4: *Your Unique Laugh* ..... p 73
Chapter 5: *Laughter And Play* ..... p 89
Chapter 6: *Laughing With Others* ..... p 103
Chapter 7: *Making Laughter A Daily Habit* ..... p 115
Chapter 8: *Laughter, Workplace Performance And More* ..... p 131
Chapter 9: *Happy Ageing* ..... p 143

PART TWO:

Support ..... p 164
Final Words ..... p 173
Quotes By Sam Rehan ..... p 174
Get In Touch ..... p 177
Acknowledgments ..... p 179
Chapter Notes ..... p 184
Research, Resources And Recommended ..... p 203

ABOUT SAM REHAN

Sam cares about laughter and has witnessed its far-reaching power to provide people from all backgrounds with the momentum to move forward, whatever their life situation. A mother based in the UK, but globally active, Sam is a workplace trainer. She supports teams and individuals to access more calm, de-stress and gain more energy. Energised people are more effective, excel at work and in their relationships and are motivated to uplift others.

Sam loves travel, the outdoors and nature. Her top strengths are kindness, fairness, creativity, excellence, leadership and lastly, but not least humour! Sam has a science background, with 30-years-plus work experience and previously delivered training to professionals in over 30 countries. Sam is a motivational speaker with a keen obsession in supporting all people, to access a stronger body and stronger mind, whatever their abilities.

Get in touch, if you would like Sam to provide an energising talk or health boosting workshop. Her clients span financial organisations, law, education, health and many other sectors. Sam shares to uplift and energise everyone, with ultimate well-being techniques and straightforward science. Sam is a Professional member of The International Stress Management Association [ISMAUK], the lead professional body for workplace and personal Stress Management, Well-being and Performance.

Get in touch...be happier, more relaxed and energised to achieve more - whatever your circumstances.

laughmore@samrehan.com
www.samrehan.com

FEEDBACK FOR SAM

"I can't recommend Sam and her laughter sessions enough. I was sceptical about how helpful they would be, but after one session I was hooked. They are so therapeutic; they really help wake up my body and emotions. They are very releasing. Sam is very knowledgeable on the science behind laughter therapy and is doing some great work with the young, the elderly and the sick."

- Mother

"Felt more relaxed and felt connection with team."

- Family Lawyer

"Felt empowered to be given strategies to reduce stress and tension and ground one-self. Thank you."

- Sales Manager

"Loved seeing my boss belly laugh... never seen it before!"

- Communications Manager

"Liked Sam's interaction with the group and of course the laughter, absolutely brilliant."

- Training Facilitator

"I went to several of Sam's laughter sessions. Although I have a chronic pain condition, these sessions always raised my mood. I could be having a bad day and go to one of the sessions and come out genuinely smiling. Giggling and humming were good at times when full laughter was not possible. The other people at the sessions also seemed to be happier at the end of the sessions than at the beginning of the sessions. I would recommend that everyone tries it."

- Jo K.

"Really uplifting experience, a great mix of exercises for improving feeling of well-being. Highly recommend Sam."

- *Language and Behaviour Consultant*

"It was great fun. A great release of endorphins. Highly recommended."

- *Care Home Manager*

"Sam came to our offices and provided a well-being talk. We get a lot of speakers, but Sam's talk was well received. She made us laugh and learn."

- *Regional Director, Finance*

"I enjoyed being free to express myself. I feel very relaxed."

- *Director*

"The laughter was infectious, and I could feel the effects on my body, mind and mood."

- *Training Manager*

"It was fun, very different and relaxing too."

- *Teacher*

"Felt empowered to be given strategies to reduce stress and tension and ground one-self. Thank you."

- *Accountant*

"I attended a few of Sam's Laughter Club sessions. The sessions were great fun and, although challenging for me at times, I felt that anything was OK. That in itself is so refreshing ... to be able to be yourself whatever. Then to laugh so much ... my cheeks started aching from not using those muscles that much for a long time ... even my tummy muscles felt different. Sam facilitates the sessions in a gentle and encouraging way, often by being playful herself so giving permission for you to also 'let go'. When I remember her classes and all the useful tips, I start to smile. I feel so good laughing just to laugh and feel great. Thank you for your enthusiasm and inspirations."

- *N. W., Health Practitioner*

"I had so much fun at Sam's laughter workshop. Sam's interactive activities lifted our hearts and our minds. What a fabulous start to our day. Thanks, Sam, for an amazing time."

P. M.

"My partner and I had a couple's laughter session with Sam. It was incredible! N. was really apprehensive at first but within a few minutes he was proper belly-laughing! It was deeply connecting, fun and I'm so glad we did it! Highly recommend it."

- Singing Teacher

DEDICATIONS

This book is dedicated to YOU my reader. Thank you for spreading goodwill and good cheer through the power of YOUR genuine smile and laughter. Keep going.

To my two children. Eshan and Roma, who inspire me, make me smile, laugh and help me do better every day. For Steve, "Once upon a time there was a girl who loved a boy and his laughter was a question, she wanted to spend her whole life answering" (Nicole Krauss). With great gratitude to my mother, who shares her joy and smiles widely.

DISCLAIMER

Names and identifying details have been changed to protect the privacy of individuals who have shared their stories in this book.

The author is not a medical practitioner and does not purport to give medical advice. The information is this book is not intended as a substitute for medical advice or to replace medication or treatment. If a reader is in any doubt as to whether to adopt any recommendations made in this book, on account of an existing medical condition or health concern, they should seek advice from a health practitioner. The reader should consult a medical practitioner in matters relating to any symptoms that may require diagnosis or medical attention.

Although the author has made every effort to ensure that the information in this book is correct at the time of going to press, the author does not assume and hereby disclaim any liability to any party for any loss, damage, or disruption caused by errors or omissions, whether such errors or omissions result from negligence, accident, or any other cause.

FOREWORD

If there was one very simple technique you could use to create contentment and happiness; to improve your mental health and lower stress levels; to enhance your performance and career; and to build stronger teams that connect with each other and work collaboratively to achieve common goals and increase productivity – how much would you pay to get your hands on it?

Now, if someone says that you can have all of the above just by understanding the power of a smile and laughing, would you believe them? Well, when I first met Sam Rehan and she spoke about laughter yoga I wasn't sure what to think. Laughter was not something that I had associated with achievement or success and it was something that belonged in one's personal life that occasionally saw the light of day. I certainly wasn't consciously aware of how powerful a resource it is. The truth is, that it is one of the hidden keys that helps us to connect with ourselves and other people and enables us to form strong bonds with each other.

We have witnessed and experienced the power of laughter within two of our organisations. The first was at one of our Connectionsb2b Business Lunch Clubs where a group of around 40 people came together – many of whom were attending for the first time – and after a session of laughter yoga the commonality shared by the group during the session remained with them and they were able to network with confidence and as friends, rather than strangers meeting for the first time.

We were so impressed with the impact and success laughter yoga had at the networking group that we wanted to test it to see whether it would have the same powerful impact within our law firm when we brought two teams of 35 junior and senior lawyers together for the first time. The introductory meeting was important as we had recently acquired another law firm and we were keen for the new team to feel part of our organisation and that this was their new 'work home'.

Sam Rehan delivered her workplace laughter yoga session to an initially apprehensive group of lawyers where laughter was not part of their daily work routine. What we witnessed and experienced as Sam guided us through the exercises was a tangible sense of us all opening up from being rather reserved and feeling a little self-conscious to embracing and owning our commonality of laughter. The invisible barriers that had been in place at the start of the meeting were lowered (and in many cases removed altogether) allowing relationships to develop and the foundation of the new larger team was formed. In the workplace, building great teams is essential to the success of a business and laughter helped us take a big leap forward in creating this new team.

This book shines a light on the well-kept secret of the role laughter plays in our lives – from the benefit of a smile to the impact laughter has on team building and productivity in a business environment. Sam shows the practical benefits and steps to take to achieve more laughter in our lives and also explains the science behind why it works – from the impact laughter has on our breathing, to the chemicals released in our brain which regulate our mood and emotions.

Understanding and implementing this powerful, freely available resource will help you create the happiness and success you seek in your personal and business life. It's a foundational pillar that supports and enhances the relationship you have with yourself and others which leads to us having the life and business we desire.

Teresa J. Payne
Solicitor and Owner of Parfitt Cresswell
(www.parfittcresswell.com)
Director at Connectionsb2b and Connections Radio
(www.connectionsb2b.co.uk)
Author of *The Later Living Guide* and *The Good Divorce Guide.*

INTRODUCTION:
HOW LAUGHTER HELPED TO SAVE A MAN'S LIFE

"A book is like a piece of rope; it takes on meaning only in connection with the things it holds together."

Norman Cousins

How much did you laugh yesterday?
How much did you laugh last week?

Let me share two true stories, where laughter helped play an extraordinary part in aiding physical and mental health.

In the winter of 2015, a single mother buried her face in her hands. In the space of exactly one week a young close family member passed away unexpectedly, her young son suffered a concussion on a school trip, and she was informed that she was going to lose her job (her sole source of income) through redundancy. Adding to that, she was living as a single mother with two young children (one with regular medical needs) in temporary accommodation. She sought to seek a way to manage her overwhelming emotions after she put the children to bed. Clambering to feel lighter, she found some comedy clips but they didn't help her racing frantic thoughts. It felt like too much work to decipher the humour. The canned (taped) laughter sounded jarring to her anxious tired mind. She searched the internet and came across clips of a very young baby's gurgling and chortling. It was a magical, life-changing moment. Her whole body began to relax as she began to smile alongside the baby's beautiful natural laughter. She replayed the video clip and then played more similar videos. It was astonishing to her, how much better she felt laughing. Her mental tension lifted and she felt less stressed and more relaxed.

The single mother was me

I sought more laughter as the days progressed. Smiling and laughing helped me to distract from my worries. The laughter supported me to access a more positive headspace so I could manage life better and stay strong for me and my children. It was astonishing to me how something as simple as laughter helped me feel so much better

With a science background, I was naturally interested in research behind laughter. Decades of research and hundreds of studies showed the wide-ranging health benefits of laughter. Even smiling creates positive changes in the body. I was hooked on accessing this emotion for a better life. I sought ways to lengthen my laughter, as the research showed 15 minutes of laughter was needed for your health to benefit. During times of anxiety, I forced a smile. On one occasion, I could not smile, but I found getting up and walking around the room helped. Moving helped me raise a smile and my laughter emerged and I felt mentally and emotionally better. Once I began to laugh more and more, the laughter came easier and easier. Even thinking about laughing improved my mood. I knew that if laughter could have this impact on me, then it could on others and I needed to proactively put it in front of more people who could really benefit from it. Laughter helped me feel less stressed and more relaxed, so much so, that I became a professional laughter facilitator.

On to the second story. Let me share how with you how laughter helped save a man's life

Over 60 years ago, the Cold War was a profound time when fear and tension was heavy between the East and the West. In

1964, a young man, Norman Cousins, became ill after a stressful trip to Russia. Cousins was an American journalist, editor and advocate for world peace. He was diagnosed with ankylosing spondylitis, a painful inflammatory illness that was crippling, and at his worst, Cousins was nearly incapable of moving his jaw. Norman's doctor told him that only one of every 500 people diagnosed with this affliction fully recovers and he expected him to die within a few months. Cousins sought conventional medical treatment. He also decided that positivity was key. He spent hours each day watching funny TV and movie clips and similar 'laughing matter'. He reasoned that if stress had somehow contributed to his illness (he was not sick before the trip to Russia), then positive emotions should help him feel better. Within a few months, his symptoms began to recede and he returned to work. He claimed that ten minutes of belly-rippling laughter would give him two hours of pain-free sleep, when nothing else, not even morphine, could help him. Norman steadily got better and within six months he was back on his feet, and within two years he was able to return to his full-time job. Encouraged by his recovery, Cousins took his message to the medical community. His story inspired a number of research projects and piqued the interest of the scientific community.

"I was greatly elated by the discovery that there is a physiological basis for the ancient theory that laughter is good medicine," Cousins wrote in an article, 'Anatomy of an Illness (as Perceived by the Patient)' published in *The New England Journal of Medicine.* [1] The article became the basis for the first [2] of 25 books Cousins wrote on emotions and healing and led to his appointment at UCLA (University of California, Los Angeles). At UCLA, Cousins led a full role: he wrote, lectured medical students, assisted in clinical research and raise funds for research.

Cousins was criticised for suggesting that laughter could cure illness. Harold Benjamin (founder of Wellness Community centres in the US) said, "He would say that is absurd. What he did say is that pleasant emotions enhance physical well-being: laughter, love, success, camaraderie are all pleasant emotions. The more we can get of them, the better off we are." [3] Benjamin also disclosed that Cousins never encouraged forsaking conventional medical treatment. Instead, he encouraged patients to enhance their treatment with techniques, relating to the brain and immunity (field now known as psychoneuroimmunology), such as imagery.

One day, in 1980, a young depressed mother Flo Porter picked up the phone and called Norman Cousins. She had a recurrence of breast cancer. Porter recalled, "I told him I was 36. I had just had a mastectomy. I had two small children, and I was fearful of dying." Cousins invited her to his house. Porter said of their one-hour meeting, "He emphasised that it was important to have a good attitude; that it didn't matter what the statistics were on my chances to live. It changed my whole life." [3] Cousins received hundreds of awards including the UN Peace Medal and nearly 50 honorary doctorate degrees. He died in 1990, 36 years after his diagnosis, aged 75.

In my role as a laughter facilitator, I have supported many people – all backgrounds, with varying physical abilities – to prolong their laughter for greater well-being. I have facilitated laughter with people with dementia, disabilities, teenagers with autism, seniors, school children and in workplaces and even held a laughter session in an operating theatre with medics. Laughter is a language that we all speak and it binds people together. We feel more connected to the people we laugh with.

People shared powerful stories associated with their laughter experiences. In one of my public laughter classes, a man roared with laughter and glowed. He shared with me that aged 14, a group of older schoolgirls laughed at him. They told him that his laugh was awful. Until that moment, he laughed quietly behind his hands but now felt he could embrace his laugh fully, a full 36 years later. It was a powerful moment to watch. I facilitated a laughter session with a group of seniors and a serene-looking petite lady raised her hand. "Can I tell everyone my experience about laughter?" she asked. We listened and our mouths fell open as her opening words were, "My father slapped me when I laughed out loud as a young girl." She vowed to laugh as much as possible, and as an adult and she continues to do so with her children, grandchildren and great-grandchildren. One lady who had had a mastectomy eight days earlier, came to my group laughter session. She said she heard about the power of laughter and afterwards felt better emotionally and physically.

A lady said she had spent three years grieving after a family bereavement, but after laughing with me said she felt she could laugh without feeling guilty and felt the best she had in three years.

A man with dementia who had lost his speech, was overjoyed he could make laughter sounds. He took 30 minutes to write out five words to me ... *"Thank you for my laugh."*

Laughter is a choice I have made. When I laugh, I feel fully present. Laughter has supported me during difficult times, enhanced personal and work relationships and supported my physical and emotional health. Laughter has led me to a successful career. I support workplaces, communities and charities with relaxation and stress management with laughter. Surprisingly, more benefits of laughing daily have emerged for me. At the time of writing this book, aged 49, I have loads of energy and as laughter stimulates facial muscles, I enjoy free natural anti-ageing!

Life continues to have its ups and downs as it does for us all, but laughter is an important DAILY form of support for me and it can be for you.

Just as I complete writing this, my son, wearing headphones, watches a video clip and is overcome with huge belly-splitting laughter. I laugh along while he remains blissfully unaware. I think I have the best job in the world.

I invite you to explore laughter with me.

"Laughter is a healthful link between surviving and thriving."

Sam Rehan

PART ONE

WELCOME TO LAUGH MORE

"The more that you read, the more things you will know. The more that you learn, the more places you'll go."

Dr Seuss

Am I happy all of the time? No and I don't think there is anybody who is. Experiencing a range of emotions is normal and healthy. But smiling and laughter are powerful resources to support us, so we can cope and struggle less. Both laughter and smiling can be used as a vehicle to change the way we think, respond and aid you towards more support and well-being.

Positive psychology can be defined as "The study of conditions and processes that contribute to flourishing or optimal functioning of people, groups, and institutions." [1] Positive psychology works by improving on what is already there and extends its help by growing and maintaining inner strengths to deal with difficult situations, challenges and normal daily life. **Laughter fits this.**

Dip into this book or read straight through. I have provided information so it is accessible, easy to digest so you can gently move towards more laughter at your own pace. This book has a wealth of knowledge, to allow you to tap into your well of options and possibilities, for a happier and healthier and successful you.

For you, I hope this book is a great source of learning, where you can get curious, make new discoveries and become more familiar with new experiences such as laughing longer, smiling more and even more. More so, my wish is that you gain understanding and can access the wide range of health benefits, along the way and long after you complete the book.

Self-reflection

Did you know that you are likely to have over 50,000 thoughts a day? [2]. Over half are negative and over 90% are just repeating from the day before.[3] Why do you think, say and do certain things? Looking inwards or self-reflection helps you gain better understanding and familiarity with your inner self. This book contains helpful self-reflection questions. Sometimes the answers come right away, and sometimes they will come later. Such questioning can help you to develop your skills and review the choices you make and perhaps shown a new direction, towards new learnings, insights, action, commitment and more support. Perhaps on a journey to a happier and healthier you.

The power of learning whatever your age

In this book, there is ample opportunity to learn if you choose. What does learning do for you? Just as physical exercise builds your muscles, when you're learning the nerve cells in your brain are growing and are developing more connections. Learning helps rewire your brain (neuroplasticity) and learning aids your memory. Evidence suggests that adult learning has a positive impact on self-esteem and confidence.[4] Even more exciting is that learning something new in one area of our life can trigger ideas in another and expand our creative sparks for more success. Every new skill you learn makes you a more well-rounded person. It creates more common ground and helps you to relate to a larger number of people in general. This can come in handy in a variety of situations, from collaborating with others at work, to more fulfilling personal relationships. Learning something new will likely make you happier, especially when it's about laughter.

Practical exercises

The *frequency* of your positive experiences is a much better predictor of your happiness than is the *intensity* of your positive experiences. [5] When we think about what would make us happy, we may think of special events, such as a surprise party, a wonderful holiday or special meal or big family gathering. But it has been shown that the key is how many good experiences you have rather than how good your experiences are. If you have a number of positive joyful experiences each day, you are more likely to be happier than somebody who had an amazing thing happen a few months ago. This book aids you in having many positive experiences each day if you create habits outlined in the exercises provided.

While reading and absorbing information in this book supports learning, putting new knowledge and skills into practice can be one of the best ways to improve learning. If you want to gain maximum knowledge and skills, then this book requires you to take some action in the form of practical exercises. These are strategies, like positive psychology interventions or PPIs. PPIs can be defined as raising positive feelings, positive thoughts, and positive behaviour. Positive psychology interventions have two essential components: focusing on enhancing happiness through positive thoughts and emotions and sustaining the effects for the long term. [6]

The exercises outlined can be viewed as intentional activities, practices in which people can choose to engage, but also require some degree of effort to participate, meaning you have to do the activity, it won't happen by itself. My experience of life has shown me that circumstances happen to people, and activities are ways that people act on their circumstances to move forward. Intentional activity can influence well-being. [7]

I have included many exercises which I do daily and teach clients, based on laughter and smiling and twinned with other PPIs such as gratitude. A greater increase in overall happiness is more likely if you practise multiple positive activities. Daily practical action creates small incremental changes over a long period of time and is key to a lifetime of greater happiness.[8] How much should I aim to laugh during the exercises? The research points to a minimum of 20 minutes of belly laughter to get a wide range of health benefits, which is a lot of laughter and easier with company. However, genuine smiling and any real amount of laughter will help you move towards more relaxation, calm and a positive state of mind. Aim to genuinely laugh as much as you can, without any discomfort or pain. Please stop and seek medical advice if laughter causes any pain.

Laughter is not always easy for many of us.

When laughter is difficult, please refer to the Support Section at the back of this book.

My intention is that this book lengthens your laughter and lightens your load.

"Daily practical action creates small incremential changes...and is key to a lifetime of greater happiness"

Sam Rehan

CHAPTER 1
WHY LAUGH MORE?

"A good laugh and a long sleep are the best cures in the doctor's book."
Irish proverb

Questions are powerful. When you ask a question, your brain works differently. [1, 2] Humans are reactive by nature and we tend to go where life takes us. But stopping to ask questions allows you to see more options, gain clarity and have greater chance for success, with your choices and goals. Answering 'Why Laugh More?' can help you look at laughter in a new way and encourage you to take action, however big or small to move forward. [3] Perhaps you can laugh more for your health, relationships and more. When you have a very meaningful why, you will do almost anything.

The charity Action for Happiness looked at research and found ten areas that make a big difference to people's happiness and which are within our control.[4] **Laughter (and smiling) fits into eight of these areas...**

1. Giving

"It was only a sunny smile, and little it cost in the giving, but like morning light it scattered the night and made the day worth living."
F. Scott Fitzgerald

Acts of giving and kindness – small and large – are associated with positive mental well-being. Research into the brain has shown that giving and cooperating with others can stimulate the reward areas in the brain, helping to create positive feelings.[5] Helping others boosts our happiness as it improves our mood and reduces stress. Supporting another helps to take our minds off our own troubles and provides a sense of meaning, and when we use our skills we can gain satisfaction. Giving can take many forms, from small everyday acts as simple as a smile. Smile and you are sharing your optimism and good attitude with others. Radiating positivity provides an optimistic worldview and a reminder to others who may be upset or unhappy to persist through adversity.

DID YOU KNOW? Happiness is recognised much FASTER than fear.[6] Smiling is said to evolve as a way to indicate that one is trustworthy and reliable. Research has shown that people are incredibly perceptive when it comes to reading and recognising different type of smiles in social situations.

2. Connect with people

"Laughter is the closest distance between two people."

Victor Borge

We need human connection as much as we require food, water and warmth. Most of us feel safe and comfortable when we're sharing strong emotions and stories. If we have good relationships, we are more likely to be happier, healthier, and live longer.[7] Laughter connects us all, as it is universal language that we all speak and understand. Laughter sounds similar across different countries and cultures, so it's immediately clear that the sound actually is laughter. When we laugh together, the shared laughter signals that we are viewing the world in the same way, and this strengthens our relationships. Connecting with someone, even briefly, can give us support to keep going and contributes our need for community. When we laugh together, there is no pecking order, we are all at the same level. Learning about laughter supports relating to people from all cultures. No matter where you are in the world, you can communicate at least a little with a giggle or a chuckle. We share our laughter when we trust each other. And laughter encourages more trust. Laughter can increase one's social support and connection with others, which in turn may improve health for all ages. [8]

3. Take care of your body

There are decades of evidence to show that laughter has positive, measurable effects on certain aspects of health even though there are not enough research findings to suggest that laughter is an all-around healing agent.

We know laughter feels good, but did you know that laughter has a long-documented list of positive mental and physical benefits that can be easily harnessed for better health? [9]

Laughter can lead to direct changes in physiological (body) systems, and this can have a beneficial effect on health in numerous ways. There is a scientific field of laughter medicine research and exploration on how laughter impacts health and disease. Hundreds of scientific studies show the wide-ranging health benefits of laughter. Some of the research findings:

- 39% decrease in stress simply anticipating humour. [10] Laughter relaxes the whole body and triggers the release of stress-releasing happy chemicals (endorphins).
- Laughter for better sleep.[11]
- Laughter and humour have been described as good complementary and alternative medicines for dementia patients. [12]

- Laughter support the body's defence against infections. Laughter reduces levels of certain stress hormones, which suppress the immune system and are associated with an increased production of cells that help to ward off infection [13]
- Prolonged belly laughter brings increased oxygen intake to support health. A longer exhale removes stale air and the inhale that follows then fills the lungs with fresh air and more oxygen [14, 15]
- Laughter for a healthy heart. The American Heart Association recommends laughter for a healthy heart, adding that research has shown laughter promotes reduced artery inflammation and increased production of HDL, or 'good' cholesterol.[16]
- Laughter for pain relief. Participants who watched comedy videos needed less pain medication. Laughter can help those suffering chronic pain. [17]

Many doctors and psychiatrists are becoming more aware of the therapeutic benefits of laughter and humour. Five hundred academics from different disciplines belong to the Association for Applied and Therapeutic Humor, dedicated to the study and application of humour to effect positive change: "The strategic use of humour sparks connection, increases influence, improves communication and can be used as a competitive advantage in any industry. What's more, humour provides innumerable benefits to our overall health and well-being, including reduced stress, greater resilience, decreased depressive symptoms, and even increased pain tolerance." [18]

4. Stop and take notice (mindfulness)

"Breathing in, I calm body and mind. Breathing out, I smile. Dwelling in the present moment I know this is the only moment."

Thich Nhat Hanh

Most of us rush through life without stopping to notice much. Slowing down and paying more attention to the present moment can be described as 'mindfulness'. Noticing your thoughts and feelings and to the world around you can help you enjoy life more and improve your well-being. And laughter is very mindful. [19] When we laugh, we are fully present feeling joy. We cannot laugh and be angry at the same time. Laughter is a form of meditation in motion.

5. Continued learning

"An intelligent person, looking out of his eyes and hearkening in his ears, with a smile on his face all the time, will get more true education than many another in a life of heroic vigils."*

Robert Louis Stevenson (*hearkening = to listen)

Just like food nourishes our bodies, information and continued learning nourishes our minds. Acquiring new information gives us a feeling of accomplishment, boosts our confidence and supports us when we face unexpected changes. Research has shown laughter supports learning: as we laugh, we relax, our anxiety decreases and our capacity to retain information expands. Laughter promotes learning, discovering, and creativity by motivating learners to engage. Laughter and humour encourage positive feelings when pursuing education and expansion of our skills. [20]

6. The ability to cope when things go wrong: resilience

"Trouble knocked at the door, but, hearing laughter, hurried away."
Benjamin Franklin

Resilience comes from the Latin word resilio – to jump back – and is used to describe our ability to cope with and bounce back from challenges. Even in the most difficult of times, humour is a wonderful way to reduce stress and anxiety, and increase your resilience and ability to cope. We can develop and improve our resilience and laughter has been found to boost resilience. Humour has been found to be associated with the development of personal resilience, and learning to laugh at yourself can improve your health and self-esteem. [21]

Life challenges, illnesses, change, loss and disappointments all contribute to stress, where the demands of the situation can exceed our resources. Humour is a valuable resource and resiliency when faced with short- and long-term stress. The ability to smile or even laugh, when times are hard, can go a long way in improving your mood and access an optimistic outlook and renew hope. In times of stress, smiling and laughter can provide breathing space for more security and strength to spring forth. Laughter has also been found to help us to focus on solutions to problems and challenges, and achieve more productive outcomes. [22]

Learning to laugh at ourselves is powerful, it not only helps us to become more resilient and forgiving of ourselves but more compassionate to others. Laughing with others can give us much needed support by another human being or a community of people where we can share our stories and burdens.

7. Positive emotions

"The face of a truly happy man seldom lacks smiles."

Ogwo David Emenike

What are emotions? In simple terms, something happens in your environment and your brain interprets it with an attitude or response. Positive emotions are emotions that we typically find pleasurable to experience and laughter can stop distressing emotions as you can't feel anxious, angry or sad when you're laughing. Laughter can lead to more positive emotional states, leading to greater health. Some common positive emotions include: love, joy, satisfaction, contentment, interest, amusement, happiness and serenity. [23] Smiles and laughs have been found to occur in 16 positive emotions. [24] A regular dose of positive emotions bring us better health and generates more positive emotions. Positive emotions, like joy (generated from smiling and laughter) helps us build well-being, promote new and creative actions, ideas, and strengthen social bonds. These strengths can be stored and be drawn upon at a later time, in different emotional states, to maintain well-being. Additionally, positive emotions have been shown to increase our performance by lifting our spirits without distracting us like negative emotions do, focus and help us broaden our horizons and widen our brain's scope of focus. Laughter can help when people are uncomfortable or in a depressed mood. [25]

8. Be comfortable with who you are

Being comfortable with yourself means feeling good about who you are and accepting whatever choices you make in life. It lessens the need for comparisons, and you do things simply for you. One way to move towards and strengthen who you really are is by doing things that make you happy. When you start focusing on what you like to do, you feel more authentic (representing one's true nature or beliefs and being true to oneself). Research has revealed that feeling happy through laughter can make people feel more comfortable and make them more likely to share personal details about themselves. Comfort in who you are conveys confidence, feeling sure of yourself and your abilities. A healthy level of confidence means you are likely to make positive contributions, be more productive, motivate others and achieve goals. Smiling conveys confidence and confident people smile. Successful use of humour signals confidence and capability. [26]

Exercise: Self-reflection Break

- What surprised you in this chapter?
- How much do you laugh?
- How much did you laugh last week?
- How much did you laugh yesterday?
- What makes you laugh?

Let's move to chapter two, where we explore what laughter is and how you can start the journey to laugh more.

"Learning to laugh at ourselves is powerful, it not only helps us to become more resilient and forgiving of ourselves but more compassionate to others"

Sam Rehan

CHAPTER 2
WHAT IS LAUGHTER AND HOW YOU CAN MAKE IT A CHOICE

"When you recover or discover something that nourishes your soul and brings joy, care enough about yourself to make room for it in your life."

Jean Shinoda Bolen

"I have been grieving for three years. The loss of my mother has been devastating. Today after laughing with everyone, I feel better. I know it's OK to laugh without feeling guilty."

A. R.

Laughter is part of a universal language of basic emotions that all humans share.[1] Across the world, people make essentially the same sounds, as laughter evolved before language. Any differences in laughter across different cultures, tends to be local dialects of laughter that evolved over thousands of years. [2]

DID YOU KNOW? The branch of science that studies the effects of humour and laughter is called gelotology. [3]

One of the theories why laughter arose explains that it was a method to reduce stress, when we got unnecessarily startled. The first human laughter may have occurred as shared relief at the passing of danger (The Relief Theory). [4] Laughter continued to evolve as a way to provide positive emotions, when coming across something unexpected and different. This is apparent in babies, who tend to laugh (or cry) at anything new, and when we hear the punchline of a new joke. Laughter also grew to have a social component, as generating laughter in others results in relaxation and releases feel-good hormones, allowing bonding and acceptance into communities.

DID YOU KNOW? There have been lots of attempts to explain why humans evolved to be the species that laughs. The Superiority Theory explains the loudest laughs were originally cries of triumph made at the expense of the enemy.[4]

We laugh before we are able to speak. The first laughter appears at about three-and-a-half to four months of age. Laughter is a way for an infant to interact with the mother and other caregivers.[5] Laughter consists of gestures and sounds. When we laugh heartily, changes occur in many parts of the body. A large part of us, is involved in laughing: voice, eyes, skin, heart, breathing and digestion. The body's laughter response is similar to crying and an actor once told me that laughing lives next door to crying. [6]

DID YOU KNOW? One study looked at the sonic structure of laughter. It was discovered that laughter can be of the 'ha-ha-ha' variety or the 'ho-ho-ho' type, but not a mixture of both! [7]

Natural laughter has a firm relationship with speech

Research has found that laughter almost always occurs during pauses at the end of phrases and suggests speech is given priority. For example, a speaker may say, 'What happened yesterday? ... ha-ha-ha' but rarely 'What happened ... ha-ha-ha ... yesterday?' This strong orderly relationship between laughter and speech (like punctuation in written communication) is called the Punctuation Effect. [7]

Laughter and humour

Laughter and humour are different. Laughter is the body's response to humour. Humour can arise from processing information or playful activities without the use of jokes such as in laughter yoga. A lot of humour is derived from communication using language. Most humour follows a pattern where we think something, based on clues given to us. This is followed by further information, which shows that we were wrong (usually very wrong) with the thinking that lead to the initial conclusion and we end by usually feeling pleasure. [8] Here is an example. 'No matter how kind you are, German children are kinder...' (wordplay humour, kinder is German for children).

Humour can be physical; It can involve anything from clowns to mimes to funny facial expressions to someone falling over. Self-deprecating humour is a favourite among stand-up comedians, in which they basically make themselves the butt of a joke and are rewarded with laughs. Laughter yoga uses zero jokes but makes use of playful activities to generate natural laughter, which often is lengthened and expands due to the contagious effects with a group participating. [9]

The effects of humour are cognitive (thinking, reasoning and remembering), for example the recognition of surprise. Meanwhile, the effects of laughter are physiological (body-based), e.g. relaxation response of chemicals when you find out that the surprise is not life-threatening. Humour encourages, and laughter is one of several possible behavioural responses to that encouragement.

Laughter anchors us to the present

Laughter gives us access to the present moment. It is a form of meditation in motion; you cannot think and laugh at the same time. When we are laughing, all our problems disappear and we are taken to joy and relaxation. Laughter feels freeing.

"Laughter is a paradox. We all know it's good for us; we experience it as one of life's pleasures and a form of emotional release. Yet to be able to laugh, we must somehow cut ourselves off from feelings of love, hate, fear or any other powerful emotion." [10]

Laughter as a social language

Part of the brain that responds to laughter triggers other parts in the brain, which, in turn, generates more laughter and helps explain why laughter is infectious. [11] Laughter has been described as a social signal and aids the findings that people are 30 times more likely to laugh in social settings than when they are alone. [12] Laughter is infectious, and sound of giggles activates the same area of the listener's brain that is activated when smiling. The brain's response then helps to prepare the facial muscles for a good hearty laugh. It is widely thought that the purpose of laughter is linked to making and strengthening human connections. The more laughter there is, the more bonding occurs within the group and provides another reason why laughter is contagious.

A few years ago, a lady approached me after my community group laughter session. She looked radiant. She took my hand and said, "Thank you." She shared that today was the happiest she had felt for a long time. She whispered that grief had been a huge part of her life after the loss of her mother. She had held back feeling happy because she felt she owed it to her mother. But that day she found it easy to let laughter out (in the group session) and it felt good. Laughing freely with others helped her to realise that it was okay to move on and enjoy living.

Permission and happiness

How much do you laugh? How much did you laugh yesterday and last week?

Do you struggle with the idea of doing something for

yourself that feels good? At the beginning of my laughter and relaxation classes, I ask the attendees if they can give themselves permission to relax more and access more of their happiness. It's quite a powerful moment when we give ourselves permission.

Permission has the same Latin root word as 'permit'. They both come from permittere, which means to allow to go or pass through. There is power and success by going after whatever you want and never asking anybody for permission to do anything. This is not about discussing items with your partner or family. This is about saying YES to more joy and more connection with yourself and others. As a child, permission was sought from your caregiver(s). Now permission starts with you. We can give ourselves that permission. We can't wait for someone else. Moving forward to make a positive change can be accomplished, through choice. You may worry that you don't deserve to laugh or you can't laugh because of what is present in your life. Most of us heard messages in childhood about ourselves, work and about rest, that are not always helpful for a balanced life. The messages we receive as children are sometimes so much more powerful because, at a young age, we make our own decisions and meanings from them. I remember hearing it was great that I was always busy, helping and completing tasks. But the tasks never stopped, there were always items that needed finishing and endless lists of jobs. I didn't hear, 'Well done for stopping and resting and having fun.' As an adult, I realised I had a choice and gave myself permission to stop regularly and enjoy myself. Actually, I was a nicer, better person if I stopped and relaxed. The positives of giving myself permission and choice to do joyful things allowed me to stay the course and continue to have lots of fun.

Countless people have said to me laughing feels so fantastic, that they wish they would do more of it but life takes over. Stopping to make room for laughter (and smiles) is a choice and you can start by giving yourself permission to laugh and smile more for greater happiness and health. Happiness is a conscious choice, not an automatic response. Give yourself permission to care for you by laughing more. You deserve to take action to have more happiness in your life.

"I gave myself permission to feel and experience all of my emotions. In order to do that, I had to stop being afraid to feel. In order to do that, I taught myself to believe that no matter what I felt or what happened when I felt it, I would be okay."

Iyanla Vanzant

Exercise: Making your choice(s)

Can you choose and give yourself permission to laugh and smile more? A YES answer will lead you to making choices to support your decision. Write down what choice(s) you can now make. For example, 'I give myself permission to laugh more' or 'I choose to invite more laughter in my life'.

Exiting your comfort zone

But what if it feels strange to smile more or even laugh more? What else could be behind uncomfortable feelings?

Each of us has our own unique comfort zone. In your comfort zone, things are familiar, you feel comfortable and there are no risks. We are good at things inside of our comfort zone, but to grow and expand our knowledge and even be great, we need to exit the comfort zone. Our comfort zones will change over time based on our thoughts, actions, experiences and skill sets.

Outside our comfort zone we can discover the learning zone. In the learning zone we can grow and learn, cultivate curiosity, make new discoveries, and find even more things to enjoy. We can expand our comfort zone. The learning zone can feel less comfortable, less safe as there is more of the unknown. However, in the learning zone you can celebrate that you are getting better, gaining confidence and new skills. Questioning,

'How can I get better?' will help you move into the learning zone.

The zones vary for different situations and are individual for each person, some are more comfortable than others. Learning about laughter and choosing to laugh more can take you out of your comfort zone and into the learning zone. Expanding the comfort zone and any progress helps you find the motivation you need to take on the next challenge and learning. When you realise more of your abilities in any area (even a small one, such as smiling more), it can change the rest of you in many ways. Learning helps you discover what you don't like, what you like and what works for you.

At a relatively early age, my thirst for education outweighed the need for entertainment. Both are important, but my time in learning has led me to expand my comfort zone daily and provided much positive change in all areas of my life. Lean into learning, knowing you may need patience, and enjoy the process. Get more support if you need it. (More in the Support chapter.)

Exercise: My last learning zone journey – reflection

- When did I last push the boundaries of my comfort zone?
- What did I do, what did I learn and how did I feel?
- How many of my activities are in the learning zone?
- What else can I do to move out of my comfort zone?

Having lots of reasons to do something can move us to take action

Why do you want to do something? Why does it matter to you? Do you want to laugh more to support yourself or yourself and others? Query why you do what you do, as well as who we do it for. The answers we have for the 'Why' and the 'What', the more likely we are to take action and create balance in our lives.

Exercise: Why?

Remind yourself why you want to laugh and smile more. Earlier in this book, I described the many ways laughter supports our bodies and minds. What are your top three reasons for smiling and laughing more? For example, learning to laugh more will help me feel better and gain more confidence. Trying something new will help me grow and learn new skills. I am going to grow as a person by taking new action.

(My own favourite is: doing new things opens me to new ideas that replace the ones I currently hold and help me connect to more like-minded people and help me serve others.)

List your whys.

Do you really lack time to be happier?

When I stopped being busy, my whole life changed. Busy meant I was making progress, I was an achiever, maximising and I felt great about ticking off long lists. One day, after a nasty fall, when I was forced to stop, I had a realisation, that there were very few gaps between my project, jobs and tasks and I was finding 'things' to fill space. I had no sense of the present moment and I was caught up in proving I could do anything that I was given and everything seems like it needed to be done. I had no balance. I was a workaholic, thriving as being seen as someone who got a LOT done in a day. Being forced to stop (due to my back injury), I noticed moments of clearer thinking and feelings that felt deeper and gave me clarity. I became less busy and to my surprise, I achieved more. I saw more opportunities that were right for me. A move from being busy led me to feel freer and more fulfilled. When I identified with what mattered, versus what can wait, I became efficient with my time, allowing me to do the things I really wanted to do and I did them regularly and many daily.

Being busy can be one of the biggest excuses for not doing things that make you happy. A good question to ask is: do you want to spend your life focusing on the things you think you have to do rather than the things you want to do? Life is about making decisions. When you start doing more things that make you happy, your quality of life can improve dramatically. When you stop being busy, you prioritise more effectively; choosing the things you want to do to move forward rather than the things you feel you should do.

As I currently finish this book, I am working more than normal. It may look the same on the outside; that I have gone back to being busy. The BIG DIFFERENCE is I feel different on the inside about my relationships to my work... it feels, manageable, balanced, happy and inspired.

Exercise: Self-reflection

- What message(s) did you hear as a child about resting and stopping?
- Are they supportive or unhelpful?
- How do you feel about your daily workload? What can you let go of?

Are you at home in your body?

When we laugh, we involve the whole body, our face, our brain, our lungs, our blood vessels and more. Our mind (thoughts, feelings, beliefs and attitudes) can affect how healthy our bodies are and what we do with our physical body (what we eat, our activity levels, our posture and how we hold our body) can impact our mind. This results in a deep relationship between our minds and bodies termed the mind-body connection. Some of the clients that I work with report feeling “disconnected from”, “removed from”, “separate from”, or “unhappy with” their bodies. Their disconnect between the mind and body can result from events in life or certain feelings that have become too painful. You can move towards feeling more at home in your body (termed embodied) with many different techniques. Seek support from a licenced therapist if you need to move forward with difficult feelings. An increased ability to be in your body in the present moment and to feel all of its sensations (emotional and physical) and becoming more embodied, is very powerful for your well-being and connecting with others.

"All the organs of our body and all the emotional responses we have, share a common chemical language and are constantly communicating with one another."

Dr James Gordon
(founder of the Center for Mind-Body Medicine). [13]

Exercise: Become more embodied through dance

Find a safe space where you can dance freely and without worry. Put on a song that you love, perhaps that moves you and 'speaks' to your body. This could be music that makes you feel more powerful, confident and joyful. Dance without care and with zero rules. Let yourself go and feel the positivity. Do whatever your body wants to do and just follow it. How does it feel for you? Dance is a language, expressed in your movements and dance is the way we can express ourselves when words can be insufficient. When the body feels good, the mind does too. Dancing offers a wonderful way to express who you are, with immersion and connection of the body and mind. Your dance can lead to mental clarity and emotional stability; dancing is good for you! It releases endorphins (happy feel-good brain chemicals) and boosts your adrenaline, so you feel happier and more confident. [14]

When you make your happiness a priority, then happiness happens

"Joy does not simply happen to us. We have to choose joy and keep choosing it every day."

Henri Nouwen

Essentially you must deliberately choose to be happy and prioritise it. When you choose what you want, you change what you do. Accessing action does not mean you to become a radically different person. You don't have to change your whole life, just add tiny segments of action. Happiness is self-care and when you make it important, it will carry and go further than you can imagine. Did you know the happier you are, the happier those around you will become?

Exercise: Self-reflection

Can I choose to be happier today? If not now, then when?
What might happen if I laugh and smile more?

Consider when you know that a change you make can be far-reaching...

Research revealed that seeing a smile can help reduce aggression in others. Just by witnessing a smile, a person about to perform an act of aggression is more likely to stop this emotion in its tracks. The research involved normal adults as well as highly aggressive teens who had been referred to a youth programme, either by educational authorities or the courts. About 70% of the teens already had a criminal record. Seeing smiles on the faces of others can have a profound effect on a person's tendency toward violence or aggression – that is, as long as that person recognises the smile as one of happiness. [15]

Find a partner to keep you on track of your goals

You have chosen to access more happiness, perhaps with laughing more. One of the best ways to make progress on your choices, is to have someone to keep you on the right track. Having to answer to another person (accountability) for your actions can hugely motivate you to continue your progress and stay on course. According to research, you have a 65% greater chance of completing a goal if you commit to someone. To stay on the right track with your accountability partner, make sure you schedule reoccurring meetings where you touch base and manage each other's progress.

If you have a specific accountability appointment with a person you've committed to, you will increase your chance of success by up to 95%. [16]

Exercise: Accountability

Tell your friends what you have decided to do: perhaps you have made a choice to complete this book and its exercises within a certain time period. Ask one or more of your friends to regularly check up on you and your progress. Book appointments with them to ask them to check what has changed/improved in your life or what is affecting your goals. Take time to look back at your successes. Let positive emotions around your progress boost your motivation.

The fear of new things

Some of us like unfamiliar things and some of us less so. How do you feel about trying new things? Do you resist and often fear it? On the other hand, do you or people you know, crave new experiences, love variety and hate routine? Opening ourselves to new things such as more laughter, can often be frightening to many of us, because it's unfamiliar and we can associate unfamiliarity as not safe. But most of the things we fear don't actually happen and the fear is not useful. We are not great at anticipating the good things that do occur as a result of our trying something new. Fear (and stress) starts with a thought and can spiral into regular negative self-talk. We all have an inner critic. A little voice can actually be helpful and reminds us to go to bed on time so we are refreshed for tomorrow. However, this little voice can often be more harmful than helpful, as it churns up excessive negativity ('you can't do that', 'you will never finish that, you never finish things', 'you sound silly' are some examples). This is known as negative self-talk, and it can really affect us and prevent us from living our full potential. It's key to remember that thoughts and feelings aren't always reality and you can minimise negative self-talk. When you imagine laughing more, do you have negative thoughts come up? What are they saying? Catch your critic by learning to notice when you're being self-critical so you can begin to stop. For example, notice when you say things to yourself that you wouldn't say to a good friend or a child. Give your inner critic a name (mine is a lizard that sits on my shoulder named Larry!). This helps you think of your inner critic as outside of yourself and helps you realise that you don't have to agree with it, and it's easier to see how silly some of your critical thoughts can be. When fearful thoughts pop up in your mind such as 'everyone is going to think you are silly for laughing' respond to the voice in your head with one of the following or similar: 'That's not useful', or 'not true'. I like to start with saying 'Thank you for telling me, Larry' and then say 'I am doing it anyway'.

When laughter brings up bad memories

It's not uncommon for people to share with me less than happy memories around laughter, especially from childhood. Perhaps a group of children laughed at you or you were bullied and it involved laughter.

We all have stories and events that we cannot change, but

we always control how we interpret what happens to us, as well as how we respond. Negative emotions are often a strong sign that something is going unaddressed. Read the support section and seek support from a licenced therapist if you need to move forward with difficult feelings and memories.

Exercise: Expressive writing

Talking through difficult experiences with a therapist and/or supportive family and friends can be helpful to make sense of what happened and your response and reactions to those events.

Expressive writing or mindful writing is the process of writing about your thoughts and feelings linked to stressful events and is also known to promote healing and resilience. Writing (without regard to the structure of the writing) is known to have cathartic qualities, i.e. serving as a stress release: decreasing the overall amount of distress held in your body. Additionally, the conscious going over difficult experiences and your reactions to these, can promote an overall sense of emotional and mental and physical well-being. [17]

This exercise can be helpful to those who aren't suffering from ongoing mental health difficulties and post-traumatic stress disorder. If you find yourself in this category it is best to engage in expressive writing with therapeutic group or individual support.

Well done for getting this far.

On to the next chapter, where we discover the power and secrets of smiling!

"...most of the things we fear don't actually happen and the fear is not useful."

Sam Rehan

CHAPTER 3
START YOUR LAUGHTER WITH A SMILE

"We shall never know all the good that a simple smile can do."

Mother Teresa

A senior shared with me, that a man smiled at her as she passed him walking home. She failed to smile back. Later that evening, she sat feeling anxious and alone. Her thoughts took her back to earlier that day and she remembered the beaming smile she received from the stranger. She started to smile and she felt somewhat better. She told me, let people know that sometimes people cannot smile back for many reasons, but perhaps like me they can receive the gift of a smile later. The shining smile from a random stranger was a little act of kindness and it had the power to provide me support in a time of need. Sometimes all it takes to make the day better, is a smile, whether it's one someone gives to you, or one you share with another.

Laughter starts as a smile. Think of smiling as a warm-up for laughing.

Smiling is part of our nature and it is widely thought to be a universal product of human evolution rather than shaped by one's culture.

DID YOU KNOW? the smile has been described as the world's most powerful gesture? Smile and the world will smile with you. [1] When one person looks at another and smiles, a brief bond is said to be formed. In a world where social media interactions can lessen meaningful connection and perhaps lead to more loneliness, a real-life, real-time human connection with a smile has great power. Putting a smile on your face can help you project confidence even when you are not feeling particularly confident. By raising a smile you'll actually begin to feel positive emotions that'll boost your confidence and help you to overcome shyness and lessen social anxiety. [2]

DID YOU KNOW? People smile often. In a study, public smiles were counted for 15,824 children, adolescents, young adults, middle aged adults and older adults. Not all groups were found to smile equally. Younger people smile more than older people.[3]

With a genuine smile, your brain starts to feel more positive emotions. A warm, friendly smile shows you're relaxed and comfortable, which aids relationships and communication. When you smile at someone they tend to smile back as brain cells (neurons) pick up and mimic the body language and facial expressions of those around us. When you smile, you can activate a person's neurons and get them smiling too, and they start feeling more positive and feel positive around you – supportive for all relationships. [4]

A genuine smile makes others more receptive, and the more others are receptive to you, the more positive experiences you'll have with others. More positive experiences lead to less doubt, fear and insecurity. When you smile you radiate confidence and warmth, and others are more comfortable approaching and engaging with you. [5]

DID YOU KNOW? Ultrasound scanning has shown babies 'smile in the womb. Babies then normally smile after birth when they are about six weeks old. This is thought to be the case, as in the womb the baby is calm and then after birth, a baby is exposed to a new environment. [6]

Exercise: Self-reflection break

- How much do I smile?
- What makes me smile?
- In my social group, who smiles a lot?
- How does smiling make me feel?
- What helps me to smile, or makes me feel more comfortable about smiling?
- Who do I want to smile more with?
- Have I made someone smile today?

Structure of a smile

A smile can begin with your senses. Perhaps someone holds your hand, you hear something pleasant, or beautiful scent meets you. You may have a thought, an old memory comes into thought, your children as babies or a flashback to your party last year. You may want to reward another or others with a smile. You may want to signal that you are not a threat or use a smile to navigate a social group. The brain interprets the information and commands a change in the face... a muscle in the cheek (the zygomatic major) draws the lips upward. Some smiles include another muscle (the orbicularis oculi) which surrounds the eye socket, raises your cheeks, causing the subsequent laugh lines at the outside corners of your eyes. This whole process typically lasting from two-thirds of a second to four seconds. [7]

Smiling aids health

How is it that smiling reduces stress and can even be used to get you relaxed so you fall asleep more easily? Like laughter, smiling is health-boosting. When you smile you tell your brain it feels good, and when your brain feels good it tells you to smile even more. Information from the muscles in your face influences your emotional state and creates changes in the body. [8]

The nervous system is essentially the body's electrical wiring. The nervous system is made up of all the nerve cells in your body. It is through the nervous system that we communicate with the outside world and, at the same time, how many processes inside our body are controlled. The nervous system takes in information through our senses, processes the information and triggers reactions, such as making your muscles move. Neurons are nerve cells that are the basic building block of the nervous system. Neurons are similar to other cells in the human body but there is one key difference. Neurons are specialised in transmitting information throughout the body. Chemical messengers of the mind that cause emotions are called neurotransmitters. [9]

(DOSE): Dopamine, oxytocin, serotonin, and endorphins are neurotransmitters triggered by smiling

Dopamine

Associated with pleasure and need. The right amount of dopamine contributes to feelings of alertness, focus, motivation and happiness. Aside from its 'feel good' function, dopamine is involved in many body functions.

Oxytocin

Associated with a feeling of belonging. When we connect with another person through a smiling face, oxytocin is released and associated with feelings of calm, support and nurture. One of the main benefits of oxytocin is that it reduces the stress hormone, cortisol, allowing for the slowing of one's heart rate and lowering of blood pressure.

Serotonin

Associated with feeling of happiness and well-being. The majority of this neurotransmitter is found in the gastrointestinal tract (the central part of the digestive system), working as an anti-depressant by controlling your mood, bowel movements and even sleep activity. This can explain why smiling has been compared to getting a good night's sleep.

Endorphins

They help to lower your anxiety levels, promoting a greater physical and mental health. Endorphins are released when a person gets hurt, but also during exercise, excitement and laughter. In addition to blocking pain, endorphins can make people happy and produce a feeling of well-being.

What does a smile convey?

Among humans, smiling shows pleasure, sociability, happiness, joy or amusement. Or does it? Research results involving smiling have been variable because there are lots of different kinds of smiles. Not all smiles are genuine smiles of joy. Some smiles are sarcastic, some polite and some smiles beam. There are subtle differences in the dynamics of each expression, and they're hard to re-create in a lab. [10]

The most studied smile

There is only one smile that researchers consider the sole indicator of true enjoyment... a Duchenne (pronounced Doo-chen) smile is a natural smile of enjoyment. The smile is distinctive, with the mouth turning up, the cheeks lifting and the eye sockets crinkling – it is the latter facial movement that make this smile different from other types of smiles. The non-Duchenne smile doesn't reach the eyes but resides only on the lips and possibly the cheeks. [11]

When you see someone displaying a Duchenne smile, you naturally feel positive emotions for the person smiling and this particular type of smile has been studied for over a century. Brain scans revealed that Duchenne smiles produced greater activity in the region, with clear connections to positive affect. A study found that heart rates among the smiling group with a Duchenne smile stayed the lowest during stress recovery. Patients with depression showed more Duchenne smiles on their discharge interviews than during their admissions, and research involving the Duchenne smile has been used to predict marital happiness, personal well-being, and even longevity. [12, 13, 14]

Non-Duchenne smiles, can reflect a rather wide range of emotions, including pain, embarrassment, deceit and grief. Alongside the Duchenne smile, other types of smiles have been described. For example, people smile when they're embarrassed, frightened, are flirting, horrified or mortified. [15] Fewer genuine, Duchenne smiles are found when lying occurs. [16]

DID YOU KNOW? Research has shown that in infants between one and six months of age, Duchenne smiling is more prevalent than non-Duchenne smiling when infants are gazing at their mothers and when their mothers are also smiling. Among ten-month-old infants, Duchenne smiles are associated with mother's smiling approach, while non-Duchenne smiles are related to the approach of an impassive stranger. [17,18,19]

Genuine smiles are thought to serve a social purpose, and evidence suggests may be to indicate selfless concern for the well-being of others (altruism) and cooperation.[20] Another function of smiling has been discovered; viewing attractive faces activated the brain's area involved in processing sensory rewards and the activity in this region was even stronger when the face in focus wore a smile. [21]

What about fake smiles?

Most commonly, people smile when they are happy, because smiling reflects happiness. But people also smile to mask negative emotion such as unhappiness and embarrassment. Have you been told, 'Cheer up, it may not happen?' Do you put on a false smile to hide certain feelings? There's no harm in smiling, but habitually forcing your expression into the shape of a smile can have a negative effect. Research has shown that smiling to hide your negative emotions could make you feel worse. Smiling for the sake of smiling can lead to emotional exhaustion and withdrawal, with a worsening of mood. [22]

When people are shown photographs of subjects with fake and genuine smiles and are asked to spot the false and the true, the participants normally get around 60% right. [23, 24]

There is evidence that substantial minorities of people have the ability to produce a Duchenne smile deliberately and put on convincing (false) emotions in everyday life. [25]

Other smiles

We are incredibly good at reading and recognising different smiles in social situations. Researchers have noted differentiation between smiles by looking at muscle activation, body language and the chemicals released when certain smiles are used. Here are some common types of smiles...

- Reward Smiles – We use them to motivate ourselves and/ or other people. For example, when a baby unexpectedly smiles at its mother.
- Polite Smile – Used when a social situation requires a pleasant expression. Polite smiles help us maintain a kind of discreet distance between people.
- Affiliative smiles – Used as a way to connect socially, to be polite, reassure others and communicate trustworthiness, belonging and good intentions.

- Dominance smiles – To show superiority, to communicate and make others feel less powerful.

How can I raise a raise a smile when it feels difficult?

If you are faced with a difficult time it can be very hard to raise a smile. Smiling helps you to find relief from stress and the pain and allows you to remember you can still enjoy life despite what you are facing.

Firstly, sit down, which help you access relaxation. Focus on your breath, which helps you to move your attention to your body. Close your eyes if it feels comfortable and picture a positive memory of joy and happiness or think of someone you love, a family member, friend or a pet or a teacher.

The second strategy that works well is to move in any way you can, that feels good and safe. Movement can help you move towards a smile as it takes you away from your thoughts and back into your body. Choosing to walk around the room or even swaying or dancing can often help create an inner shift towards feeling better and lead to a genuine smile. If you are unable to stand or walk, shake your hands or shrug your shoulders or sway as you remain seated. I have worked with clients with very little mobility, and very slight movements moved them away from anxious thoughts to connect with their body. Perhaps a smile is not possible right now, but it is likely that the intention to smile and movement has led to you softening, feeling better and open to a smile in the near future.

Exercise: How to smile more easily... a genuine smile

What if smiling is a new habit for you, and it takes a while for positive feelings to appear, or you are faced with too much negativity? How can you move to a genuine smile more easily? Create a smile filing cabinet in your brain, with happy moments that you can recall to aid you when you wish to boost your mood with a smile. Access memories where you laughed heartily, take your top or top three songs that make you happy, add perhaps one or two funny scenes from a movie that tickle you. Recall any funny memories of family members, friends or pets that make you smile and feel lighter. File images and conversations that are full of strong positive memories. Laughter causes regions of the brain that control emotions to light up. These areas of the brain suppress the release of stress hormones and activate the brain's memory centre. This explains why so many of your most memorable moments involve laughter and happiness. You can now access the smile cabinet when you choose to lighten your load.

Here is one of my personal favourite happy memories that allows me to access a fast smile: the memory of my toddler playing with a tissue box never fails to bring a smile to my face. I found my son, aged one, pulling out a facial tissue with his left hand and then he pulled out another tissue with his right hand. Like a music conductor he flapped his hands, and one by one he pulled out ALL the tissues from the box. He smiled and laughed with glee. Now I share that memory with my teenage son and we both smile together.

Smiling and mirror neurons (a special class of brain cells)

A smile has even been described as a powerful gesture. Anyone who sees you smile often responds by mirroring the action and smiling back. Brain cells, called mirror neurons, activate when we see someone doing something and they help our brains bounce smiles from one person to the next. As its name suggests, mirror neurons enable us to copy or reflect the behaviour we observe in others and have been linked to the capacity for empathy. What makes mirror neurons so special is that they are activated both when we PREFORM a certain action; such as smiling, reaching for a cup and when we OBSERVE someone else performing that same action. Mirror neurons blur the distinction between seeing and doing. It was previously thought that our brains use thinking processes that interpret and predict other people's actions. But mirror neurons demonstrate we understand others not by thinking, but by feeling. Alongside stimulating other people's actions, we also 'get' the intentions and emotions behind those actions. When you see someone smile, your mirror neurons for smiling fire up too, creating a sensation in your own mind of the feeling associated with smiling. You don't have to think about what the other person intends by smiling. You experience the meaning immediately and easily. Humans are social beings programmed to learn from others and mirror neurons allow us to learn through imitation. They are important for relationships and enable us to reflect body language, facial expressions and emotions. Mirror neurons intervene in our daily lives, make smiling and laughing contagious and allow us to access good feelings associated with both. [26, 27, 28]

Exercise: Smile for success and connection

Gear up for success for example, **before** making a phone call, an interview or interacting with a customer or client. Recall a happy or joyful memory or event when you felt deep satisfaction. Remember an event that brought you deep satisfaction, happiness and joy. Visualise, if you can, the details, such as the people, sounds or colours associated with the memory, to enhance the feel-good sensations with the emerging smile. This will aid you to relax, create softness around you and connect you with others in a positive beneficial way. Remember, a genuine smile is the way forward otherwise it is likely the other person will notice it and it will raise suspicion and affect mutual trust.

How to get comfortable with your smile

This will help you become more comfortable with your smile and helps the act of smiling become easier and more natural.

Practise a genuine smile (the Duchenne smile) by smiling using the muscles around your eyes. Access positive happy memories from your past to help you raise a genuine smile. In front of a mirror, practise smiling with a piece of paper in front of your mouth and you'll learn to feel the difference between a fake and a genuine smile. Concentrate on your eyes. Cover the lower part of your face with a piece of paper. Picture joyful, happy moments from your past to help you raise a genuine smile. When your eyes are smiling with a genuine smile, really concentrate on what muscles are working and why, and remember this each time you smile. Try to engage these muscles each time you smile. Where possible, access feeling good and smiling rather than placing a false smile on your face.

Exercise: Regular smiles

Make a list of three things that make you smile. Can you spend more time with those things or do those things?

Find little things to smile about throughout the day. We often smile when we receive direct benefits, such as a compliment, a surprise or gifts. But what if you smiled each time you recognised all the good around you? Every time you feel grateful, thankful or appreciate someone or something, allow yourself to smile. Can you smile during the feeling of a nice, warm shower? Can a smile beckon when someone hands you a hot drink?

"I can hear birdsong. I smile because I appreciate family, food and joyful surroundings. I give thanks and smile for even the seemingly negative things that came into my life – illness, pain and loss. For these were some of the most powerful teachers and they showed me the strength and power within me to cope and it led me to my successful career."

Mother of five

How to use a smile to aid sleep

You can use a smile to peacefully fall asleep or fall back to sleep when you wake up in the middle of the night. Lying down in a comfortable position, add a slight and comfortable smile to your face. Use the muscles around the lips without straining to produce a tiny small smile. It's a very gentle slight smile that doesn't feel forced or involves any work. The smile helps both the brain and the body to relax. With actual danger, you would not be smiling and likely be on your feet, so lying down with a smile is a signal to the brain and nervous system that everything is OK, that you're safe and content. Alongside the gentle smile, you can add some easy meditation by using your breath and imagining a balloon. Relax your body and begin to take deep inhales and slow exhales through the nose. Start to take a slow, deep COMFORTABLE breath to fill your belly up with air, as if you're trying to blow up a big balloon. Expand your belly as much as you can. Slowly let the air out of the balloon (through the nose) as you release the breath from the belly. Feel your body relax each time you exhale; each time air is slowly being released from the balloon. Continue for several minutes to aid the sleep process.

DID YOU KNOW? Spend more time with people who smile a lot. Research has shown that it's very unlikely you'll be able to keep a sad face if you're looking at people who are sharing their genuine smiles with you.

I want to smile more but...

It's not uncommon for me to hear clients telling me that they would smile if only they felt better about their teeth or liked their mouth. They share their negative thoughts. One lady shared with me that she felt others would judge her on her past. "They probably think that I should have taken better care of my teeth." Here are some strategies I share that support a move towards self-acceptance.

Be aware of the thought that arises when it occurs. Can you observe them and say, 'Oh, I'm negatively thinking about my teeth again? What else am I feeling? Sad, lonely?' Thinking about it doesn't always make the feeling go away, but it can help you feel you have more control over it and view what else can be occurring in terms of needs. If you can, bring your attention to your body, when you have that thought, what sensations do you feel and where? This helps you to move away from your thoughts and into the bigger part of you, your body. It also helps you recognise that your negative thoughts are not necessarily the same as 'reality'.

Talking about it with a trusted friend can often help so the insecurity begins to lose its power.

"My close friend was genuinely surprised that I was hating my mouth. She never even thought about my mouth until that moment. Her listening helped me realise how out of proportion the voice had gotten in my head. It was good to share."

Make a choice to regularly sit with yourself and notice which physical parts of you you admire and love. Perhaps it's the shape of your ears, the size of your eyes, or your strong legs. Expand your thoughts to really acknowledge parts of you that you are thankful for. Little by little, add more of you that maybe you have never even thought about. The soft skin on your shoulders or the wonderful tummy that bore your children and even the amazing nose that warms and filters the air you breathe all the time. It's a powerful exercise that I do regularly and I recommend you do it too.

Smiling, culture and homelife

Why is smiling a key part of social exchanges in some cultures and not others? Research has shown a striking difference in how often people smile in the United States when compared to Russia. One explanation is how people in different cultures communicate with one another. The expectation of privacy in a given culture is referred to as social distance, and in Russia social distance is lower when compared to the U.S. This means Russians generally expect to be approached by strangers and there's more mutual understanding. There's less pressure to display a positive emotion like smiling to signal friendliness or openness, because it's generally assumed you're already on the same wavelength. In America, strangers approach one another less frequently and when they do, a smile can support the interaction and help the other person feel at ease. Another explanation considers cross-cultural differences in personality. [29, 30] Research compared caregivers in Russia and America and found that mothers in Russia reported that their infants and toddlers were more likely to demonstrate negative emotions, such as anger or frustration, and lower levels of positive emotional expression, including smiling and laughter. It also found the American toddlers were better at controlling their emotions and behaviours. The research leans towards saying that in Russia children may only smile when they're truly happy... an authentic expression of emotion. American youngsters may develop an understanding that smiling is an important social prompt that signals acknowledgment or appreciation of another person, rather than necessarily reflecting how they truly feel. This might explain why American children who smile more also tend to have more self-control. The attitudes and beliefs of adults could play a role. American parents may think that children who express themselves in positive ways also have other beneficial characteristics, such as the ability to focus and control their behaviour, i.e. a happy child is perceived as a 'good' child. In comparison, Russian caregivers may not see any link between a child who smiles a lot and his or her manners and behaviour. This could lead to Russian children displaying fewer smiles in everyday social interactions, as adults. [31,32]

"We had very little growing up but the main thing I remember is my mum smiling a lot and saying, 'We are not poor, we're just on a magical quest for quids'. She smiled and I never worried."

Jack R.

Exercise: Self-reflection break

- Make a list of the people in your life you remember growing up with.
- Did you grow up in a household where smiles were frequent?
- Who made you smile? What did they say or do?
- D.O.S.E.* yourself with happiness... SMILE! (*Dopamine, oxytocin, serotonin and endorphins)

Thank you for getting this far.

Onwards, where we expand our smile to a laugh.

Let's explore YOUR unique laugh.

"Make a choice to regularly sit with yourself and notice which physical parts of you you admire and love."

Sam Rehan

CHAPTER 4
YOUR UNIQUE LAUGH

Ann approached me after a well-being laughter talk at a local community event. She had previously been involved in a car accident and had lost some cognitive ability (mental capability). She shared that she was able to laugh but it felt wrong, almost like her laugh belonged to someone else. I found a quiet spot and asked if she would follow me as I showed her a laughter exercise. She did and then she exclaimed loudly, "I can feel it, I can feel MY LAUGHTER!"

(The laughter exercise I shared is described later in this chapter.)

What we find funny might vary by culture, but people across the world make essentially the same sounds with a bit of variation.[1] How do you feel about your laugh? Do you laugh out loud or giggle behind a hand? Do you laugh discreetly hiding your laugh or are you happy to release a huge belly laugh? We all have our own individual style of laughter and different laughs that we let out at different times, depending on how we feel and where we are and perhaps shaped by our upbringing. A lot of our laughter can be within the 'social masking' spectrum – that is, we laugh the way we do, to be polite or to create social bonds. [2]

Numerous words describe laughter such as cackle, chortle, chuckle, crack-up, har-de-har, hee-haw, hoot, giggle, guffaw, mirthful, roar, shriek, snigger, snicker snort, titter.

DID YOU KNOW? Mirthful laughter is described as laughter which is joyous, full of happiness, cheerful and jolly. In a study looking at stress and laughter, a Humor Response Scale© (HRS) [3] was used where 1 described 'No humour' and 7 indicated 'Nearly Continuous Laughter plus belly laughter or other spontaneous body movements'. A score of 25 or above on the HRS, indicated mirthful laughter responses, that had significantly increased cell activity that is linked to disease resistance. [4]

What causes our laughs to sound different from one another?

"A flower does not think of competing to the flower next to it. It just blooms."

Zen Shin

Laughter is extremely variable between individuals and we each have our own laughter signature. In short, our body and body systems and human behaviour cause our laughter to sound different. When we talk, we shape sound using our tongues. We have control over our mouth and our rib cage, which enables us to control the act of talking and other vocalisations, such as singing, beatboxing and throwing our voice. But laughing is a different vocal behaviour. When we laugh, the muscles between our ribs start to perform large, strong movements (contractions). These squeeze air out of you and make a noise – each 'ha ha ha' or 'ho ho ho' (depending on the shape of your mouth) in a laugh reflects one of these contractions. When these contractions start to run into one another, you may start to make wheezing sounds. As you force air out under much stronger pressure than when you are speaking normally, you may also start to produce sounds with much higher pitches than found during normal speech. If you laugh hard, you may make sounds that you never normally make. A really powerful effect of laughter is that if you start to laugh it can be excessively difficult to not go through with the laughter – it will come out one way or the other. [5]

"All laughter is unconscious," he said. "You do not choose to laugh the way you chose to speak."

Robert Provine [6]

Why do I not laugh when I try to tickle myself?

"Happiness has two hands: one with strength for lifting up heavy hearts and a gentle hand for tickling."

Richelle E. Goodrich

It appears the brain needs tension and surprise for laughter to emerge during tickling. The brain can distinguish expected sensations from unexpected sensations. If we use our hands (expected sensation) to attempt to tickle ourselves, our brain anticipates this contact from the hands and prepares itself for it. In contrast, if someone tickles us (unexpected sensation), we can experience unease and panic. It's not clear why, but laughter emerges as a natural reaction and with some people even before they are tickled. [7]

Laughter and culture

As well as being universal and natural, is laughter culture-specific?

Humour and what we find different, is. The social standards of every culture are different, for instance there are situations where to an American it would be fine to laugh when for a Japanese it would be rude. Laughter not so much. Each culture draws the boundaries between nature and culture differently...

Bushman laughter

Colin Turnbull in his fieldwork among the bushmen (or Mbuti) of southern Africa noticed that they had a distinctive way of expressing amusement and described it as thus: "When [the Mbuti] laugh, they hold onto one another as if for support, slap their sides, snap their fingers, and go through all manner of physical contortions. If something strikes them as particularly funny they will even roll on the ground... The [Mbuti]... likes to laugh until tears come to his eyes and he is too weak to stand. He then sits down or lies on the ground and laughs still louder." [8]

Iban tribe in Borneo

The explorer Redmond O'Hanlon describes people from the Iban tribe in Borneo; when they thought something was really funny and they were going to laugh for a long time, they would prepare by lying down first. In his book, Into the Heart of Borneo, O'Hanlon describes how he did something comedic, and turned around to see both locals in the process of lying down. He writes, that he heard "a weird gurgling sound" and turned to look at his three native guides. "The Iban, when they decide something is really funny, and know that they are going to laugh for a long time, lie down flat first." [9]

Fake laughter and cultures

People across cultures and continents are largely able to tell the difference between a fake laugh and a real one. It has been found that participants from smaller, less industrialised societies tend to be more accurate in identifying fake laughs. This suggests that in places where deep and complex social relationships are critical to survival, people are more familiar to the emotional engagement of others, and hence more likely to use those signals to predict other people's behaviour. [10]

Inappropriate laughter

"Thank you, thank you. For 30 years, I have hated myself for laughing as a teenager at my Gran's funeral. Now you have explained it, I feel a burden has lifted. It wasn't my fault."

Grandmother

After nearly every public, community or workplace laughter session, at least one individual has approached me and, with an ashen face or looking embarrassed, asked/whispered, "Why did I laugh?" or "I heard someone laughing during a funeral". The laughter that arose was during a solemn part of the service and not a reading where interesting and fun moments from the life of the deceased were shared. All emotions are expected and normal in the grieving process. A funeral can be very stressful. And most people don't go to funerals very often, and when they do it's either part of the grieving process, saying goodbye, or supporting a friend or relative who is grieving. Laughter when something is sad, can be a means of deflecting going deeper into your emotions and may be an unconscious process that is occurring, not necessarily a conscious one. In other words, your mind is finding a way to combat overwhelming emotion and it's normal. In some cases, laughing is letting off steam. For some, the tension of the moment is so high that laughter is the only release they have available. It feels as if the body in a split second chooses laughter instead of crying and it can shock us. For some, difficult moments bring sudden laughter out of nowhere, and it seems highly inappropriate to others. Laughter may have emerged in humans to cope with unexpected events and may explain why. For most of us, funeral attendance is not a normality and is out of place, which brings up laughter due to our evolutionary past. Laughter is not intended to show disrespect. It is simply one person's way of handling stressful situations. Sometimes you cannot help but laugh. If it is inappropriate, people will either understand or they won't. Don't let it keep you from living. [11]

Laughter and judgement

Laughing together builds connection, trust and community and helps us to forget worries and pain, even if only for a short time.[12] Being laughed at is altogether another matter. It can lead people to become anxious, fearful and wonder whether there's something wrong with them and they can start to question personal qualities. We've all likely had the experience of being laughed at by our friends, co-workers, family members and even strangers... some more than others.
Here are some of responses I have received from clients, when I asked about being laughed at:

- I find the best way to help or 'get over' people laughing at you is to laugh with them. It releases your energy and disarms them of their power directed at you.
- I think that you should focus on gaining more confidence so that even if they are actually laughing at you, you are also having fun.
- I remind myself that they are not laughing at me, they are laughing at the funny situation. They think it's harmless to laugh, so I laugh as well.
- Reframe it. Search for the reasons you think they would be laughing at you and challenge them. For example, 'they are laughing at me because I'm not as clever as them.' A challenging thought to this would be 'how do they know that? And even if they do think so, why should this affect me?'
- What works for me is that I try to ignore them. Normally I feel so self-conscious but know it will pass. Luckily, it doesn't happen often.
- One member of the extended family laughs at my expense. I am shy and it bothers me more than he realises. I am going to enlist my sibling to help by having a word because it's affecting me.

- What I remembered was that they are probably also worried about being laughed at too. Good to know you are strong and can do anything you put your mind to.
- If you feel stressed when it happens, remember that others are probably more concerned just as much with themselves as you are with yourself. It helps to accept that it's their choice and realise that it doesn't make them correct in doing so or reflect badly on you.
- People often laugh at me and the best way that I have found to get over this is to build my self-confidence. I know my strengths and use them as my advantage. Embrace you, you are special.
- We need to laugh about ourselves sometimes. Remember the most important thing is our own beliefs. People can hurt but only we can choose what we believe about ourselves.
- When you make up your mind that you just don't care either way. Trust me you'll be 100% better.
- Remember they are only human too and not more than you. If we allow them to get us down by feeling like their entertainment then that would be defeating the purpose of equality because even if you feel they are laughing at you, that says more about them then about you.
- I know it's easier said than done but let it roll off your back. People will laugh and be mean but, in the end, if they see it's not bothering you, they will get bored with it and leave you alone. So, act like you couldn't care less and it won't be fun for them anymore.
- Move away from your thoughts and look around, everything is much more at peace than your mind makes it out to be. Take a deep breath and reassure yourself that what happened is now passing.
- Kind human beings don't go around hurting others for no reason. I wish them well because they must be hurting to do that to someone.

- If you feel like other people are laughing at you it might be due to negative self-image. People are so preoccupied with themselves they barely can pay attention to others. To get over that feeling you need to change the way you talk to yourself in your head. Focus on all your positive qualities.
- I move away. If someone makes me uncomfortable, I leave the conversation and find someone else to talk to. I don't engage in unfunny conversations.

Explore your laughter with silent laughter!

I have great success with authentic laughter emerging with the following playful exercise... silent laughter. Silent laughter is a form of laughing yoga (zero yoga poses but hearty breathing) and can reduce stress and promote a positive mood. Silent laughter is essentially a deep belly laugh without using your vocal cords. I have used this exercise with people from all backgrounds and ages.

Exercise: Silent laughter

Find a place where you will not be disturbed. Standing up or sitting down, give your body, hands and legs a shake. Notice your breath. Now laugh as loudly as you can **without making a sound.** You can move and make playful actions as you laugh widely BUT SILENTLY, without a single sound! You may choose to take it a step further (like I do sometimes!) and roll on the floor as you make laughter (silently). Stop, take a few breaths and follow by **laughing out loud, as loud as you can or want.** Initially, not being able to laugh with sound, in the first part, usually makes you want to laugh a lot when you laugh out loud in the second part... often wonderful authentic laughter emerges.

Do you feel vulnerable when you laugh?

"When we were children, we used to think that when we were grown-up, we would no longer be vulnerable. But to grow up is to accept vulnerability."

Madeleine L'Engle

"I feel I can't hide when I am laughing. I like it but it's a bit scary."

Sara age 21

To be vulnerable means to put ourselves in a position that could potentially hurt us. We fear, because somewhere in our lives, we've been hurt before, a heart break, a rejection or a criticism and we want to avoid situations that could cause us the same pain again. Perhaps we were laughed at by a group of children or somebody made fun of us in a workplace and even loved ones. Whether we mean to or not, we're all constantly judging each other, and the sound of our laugh is no exception. The way we laugh, something we think of as happening outside our control, isn't safe from scrutiny from ourselves and others.

Letting ourselves feel happy through laughter is often a way to feel more vulnerable. Some of my clients have described laughing in public like singing... petrifying and exposed.

"I feel fantastic. I was really worried about laughing in a group, but the fear went once I realised I was having so much fun and everybody was laughing with me."

Father, aged 43

Taking the plunge to laugh openly in a group means being braver and this leads to more possibilities and opportunities with others and in life. Being vulnerable and allowing our full laughter to emerge, gives us and others access to the honest parts of us. Many of us walk round with a large part of us closed off. Laughter helps us to reveal more of us and move people to do the same. When you show someone your truer self, as with laughter, you invite trust. People relate that we are being braver and they connect to that.

People can be uncomfortable with vulnerability in others, either because it forces them to feel their own vulnerability (which can feel very uncomfortable), or because they feel a responsibility to make the other person's vulnerability go away and are unable to do so. Laughter is useful as long as it is not mocking or laughing at another. If you are on the end of a mocking sort of laughter, walk away every time. Those who use unkindness to shield themselves against their own vulnerability are best avoided.

"If there's a feeling you have, other people have it. If there's something weird about your life, other people have lived it. If there's something kooky about your body, other people have that, too. We're not alone. There's some kind of tremendous relief in that and I think it can only be expressed in belly laughter. This tremendous relief that happens the millisecond we realise, it's not just me. That's what good laughter is about. It's about knowing that you're not alone." Brené Brown [13][14]

Caution... forcing vulnerability

Real organic vulnerability jumps out. A person shines, is in the moment and shares a true part of themselves, for example a burst of laughter without expectation. The opposite can happen. I have attended numerous workshops where sharing and connecting is expected. I have witnessed individuals expressing not because they want to but feel obliged to. Vulnerability leads to meaningful deep connection so there is a want to create it. When it's not real authentic organic vulnerability, we can feel closed off. An expectation to open up, when we are not ready is not helpful and can create stress and further barriers. With my client work (individual and group), I offer an unconditional way out. At any point, a participant is free, without reason to step out and withhold answering.

In personal interactions, I pause and if I feel I am being pushed to share (even if it is from a good place), I respond by saying 'Thank you for asking. I am going to choose to opt out from answering because that's how I feel right now". Sometimes, I need to repeat this statement twice if the listener prompts again for a response.

Exercise: Vulnerability

Look at yourself in the mirror. Focus on your breath for a minute. Smile (use a positive memory or picture to access a genuine smile). If it is difficult to smile, choose to look away briefly and then look back in the mirror. Tell yourself, 'I am open to be the truest version of myself.' Breathe, smile and repeat. A wonderful exercise to do daily.

Exercise: Self-reflection break

- Do I share the same sense of humour with my parents?
- How do I feel about the sound of my laugh?
- Do I laugh fully or hold back laughter?

Laughter, pain and stress

"Sometimes, allowing yourself the time, and room, to see the humor in some of life's lighter moments can bring levity to stressful situation. In those moments, choosing to laugh is like a booster shot to your resilience, with no unpleasant side effects and hopefully some unexpectedly pleasant ones."

Cancer Treatment Centers of America [15]

A difficult time, a bereavement, a worrying health diagnosis such as cancer are not laughing matters. Laughter can and often is a resource we can use to provide us with respite and support and allow patients, carer and anybody, to find relief from stress, pain and the discomfort of medical treatments. Laughter inspires hope and connects you with others in a deep meaningful way. Such is the power of laughter, that laughter and humour facilitators are booked to provide sessions in many clinical settings all around the world.

"Humor provides innumerable benefits to our overall health and well-being, including reduced stress, greater resilience, decreased depressive symptoms, and even increased pain tolerance."

The Association for Applied and Therapeutic Humor.[16]

Humour helps create distance from our everyday challenges, creating a more positive attitude and resilience to continue even with continuous pain. Many research studies validate the pain-relieving effects of laughter. The most pain-relieving type of laughter is prolonged laughter using belly laugh... as little as 15 minutes of laughter has shown to increase pain tolerance by 10%. If it's difficult to laugh for whatever reason, watching a comedy film encourages production of your own pain-reducing endorphins (happy chemicals). [17] Clients in chronic pain have shared that constantly coping with pain, hiding its intensity from others, is often a life full of fear and stress. They seek out laughter as anything which can reduce strain and make life seem brighter and lighter is essential. Laughter is a powerful medicine and laughter has shown to help cope with chronic illness. Laughter accompanied by joy and relaxation is key in lowering pain levels, together with a happy cocktail of chemicals that are released to aid health. Do seek out laughter as a possible resource to manage your condition and pain. Spend time with people who laugh easily and who are playful... both are contagious and connecting with others is essential to your well-being.

"I was feeling really down because of the pain and stress in my life right now. So, I took your suggestion and looked up a comedy programme and found an old comedy sketch that had me in stitches! It was a wonderful feeling to let things go for a few minutes! Thank you."

Laura, aged 42

Be aware that not everyone is in the mood for humour so take into account the sensitivity of others. Individual differences dictate that humour and, as with all communication behaviours, must be employed mindfully.

"I think laughter is so important, and beneficial, but you can't take it like a pill. That's part of the problem of humour in a therapeutic context."

Dr Peter Spitzer[18]

Laughter professionals

The use of laughter professionals, rather than relying on the medical and nursing staff to raise laughter, is advantageous. Laughter facilitators are often versed in how to raise natural laughter and work carefully when working in a person's space. It is also important to be aware of the patient's condition so laughter remains comfortable and safe. Laughter allows people to remember they can still enjoy life and have fun despite challenges. Patients who have experienced laughter facilitation yoga/therapy say that it provides them with a time and space where they don't think about their diagnosis and gives them time to reconnect with joy.

Laughter yoga is a laughter-based exercise routine and well-being workout developed by Dr Madan Kataria[19] and has been used to look at how it can be helpful for cancer patients. Cancer is usually accompanied by considerable stress for the sufferer, and the stress has destructive effects on the chemotherapy treatment process. Laughter yoga has been shown to decrease the stress in cancer sufferers before chemotherapy. [20]

"Laughter Therapy is a type of therapy that uses humor to help relieve pain and stress and improve a person's sense of well-being. It may be used to help people cope with a serious disease, such as cancer. Laughter therapy may include laughter exercises, clowns, and comedy movies, books, games, and puzzles. It is a type of complementary therapy. Also called humor therapy."

The National Cancer Institute (NCI)
Dictionary of Cancer Terms [21]

Medical professionals and laughter as a coping mechanism.

One hundred and forty-two nurses described how they used humour to relieve job tensions. 21% reported using humour most often during 'patient care' situations such as providing medicines, moving patients, physical therapy, and so on. More than one third reported using 'word-play/language' as a humorous coping strategy.[22]

"In the practice of oncology, I have found that a major source of joy comes from laughing with my patients. I have found humor to be tremendously useful when used at the appropriate time and in an insightful and sensitive manner. It connects patient and oncologist on multiple levels and provides levity and stress relief in difficult circumstances. It is also a powerful tool to alleviate the emotional burden of being an oncologist."

Suneel D. Kamath, MD [23]

Exercise: Crossover laughter

*This is the exercise I used with Ann at the start of this chapter Use your left hand to pat your right shoulder and use your right hand to pat your left shoulder (or left hand to right knee or right hand to left knee). As you pat, add the following sounds with a smile: 'ha ha ha, ho ho ho'. Follow by adding a gentle or loud laugh as you pat your body as described. Movement involving opposite sides of the body working together are called contralateral movements and they help the right and left sides of the brain to work together. Additionally, touch aids circulation in the body and often brings reassurance and calm.

Are you good at laughing?

When you do things, you're good at, you feel good. It doesn't matter what it is, but the more worthwhile we consider something, the better we feel when we're good at it. If you think that laughing is important for health and connection, and that you're good at laughing, then acknowledging you are good at laughing increases your self-confidence and is a great reminder to do more of it.

Well done in getting this far.

The next chapter helps you to explore your laughter further and perhaps if you think you are not good at laughing... it will demonstrate you are!

"Spend time with people who laugh easily and who are playful..."

Sam Rehan

CHAPTER 5
LAUGHTER AND PLAY

"The body heals with play, the mind heals with laughter and the spirit heals with joy." Proverb

It is stated that humans are the only mammals who no longer play in adulthood,[1] but research shows that play boosts a positive mindset, makes us feel both happier and more inventive.[2]

Did smiles and laughter emerge from play signals?

Playfulness emerges in the laughter work I do and promotes more laughter. But there is play without laughter and laughter outside of play. There is a strong theory that laughter evolved as a play signal.[3]

In conversations, we may switch from serious discussion to making funny comments and continue to keep the same vocabulary and grammar. This similarity between non-serious and serious language and actions can be distinguished by play signals. The oldest play signals in humans are smiling and laughing. According to ethologists (dealing with human character and with its formation and evolution), these evolved from similar play signals in pre-human apes.

Mock-aggression is said to be the earliest form of play, from which all other play developed. It was critical that all participants were aware that the playful activity was not real aggression, otherwise an animal might respond with deadly force. It is speculated that the first play signals in humans evolved from two facial displays (still found in gorillas and chimps).

One was the 'grin face' where the corners of the mouth and the lips are pulled back to expose the gums, the jaws are closed, there are no vocal sounds, body movement is inhibited, and the eyes are directed toward an interacting partner. This 'silent bared-teeth display' evolved into the human social smile of appeasement (non-resistance).

In the second facial display, the lips are relaxed and the mouth open, and breathing is shallow and like panting. This vocal sounds in chimpanzees is on the in-breath: 'Ahh ahh ahh.' This 'relaxed open-mouth display' or 'play face' is said have evolved into human laughter. The relaxed mouth in laughter contrasts with the mouth in real aggression, which is tense and prepared to bite hard. That difference, combined with the distinctive shallow, rhythmic breathing pattern, distinguishes laughter as a play signal: 'This is just for fun; it's not real fighting.' Hence laughter is said to have evolved to produce positive reactions from other people and to communicate to them that we mean them no harm.[4]

Tracing laughter to a play signal in early humans fits in with young children today, who laugh during the same activities (chasing, wrestling and tickling), in which chimps and gorillas show their play face and laugh-like vocal sounds.

Males and aggressive humour

The idea that laughter and humour evolved from mock-aggression, could also help explain why so much humour today, especially in males, is playfully aggressive. Men naturally make more jokes, which tend to be in the form of aggressive banter, according to Professor Sam Shuster. As part of his research, the professor rode a unicycle around Newcastle upon Tyne and judged the reaction of 400 onlookers. He said men were much more likely to yell out at him, and when they did 75% of them made snide jokey comments such as 'Lost your wheel?'

whereas women tended to make encouraging remarks and were much more likely to praise his skill and show concern for his safety. His findings support the theory that men are more likely to use humour aggressively by making others the butt of the joke. "The idea that unicycling is intrinsically funny does not explain the findings," said Professor Shuster. The simplest explanation, he says, is the effect of male hormones such as testosterone.[5, 6] He said, "At 11–13 years, the boys began to get really aggressive. Into puberty, the aggression became more marked, then it changed into a form of jokes." This evolved into what Professor Shuster describes as adult male humour, "repetitive, humorous, verbal put-downs, concealing a latent aggression." But the jokes diminished with age, with waning testosterone levels, as older men responded more neutrally.

The power of play as adults

"We don't stop playing because we grow old; we grow old because we stop playing."

George Bernard Shaw

How do you feel when you hear giggling, and uninhibited screams of joy from children playing with complete abandonment? Do you want to participate? Do you hark back to the days when you played carefree and when life was about having fun and enjoying ourselves?

Many words can be used to define 'Play': to amuse oneself, wield lightly, keep in motion, a 'state of being', purposeless, fun and pleasurable; to exercise or employ oneself in amusement, or recreation and to do something in sport that is not to be taken seriously. Play could be anything where we are having fun, feeling light and joyful. [7]

- Board games, activities or sports
- Sharing jokes with a co-worker

- Throwing a ball on the beach
- Dressing up on Halloween with your kids
- Building a snowman in the yard
- Playing fetch with a dog

Play matters, no matter how old you are. As adults we have responsibilities, caring, completing tasks and chores, personal and professional responsibilities and we can surround ourselves by seriousness. Play can be perceived as unproductive, frivolous or even a guilty pleasure. We associate play with childhood, and therefore 'playing' with childishness. But play provides restful respite from work.

Science has found adults benefit from play in a number of ways and is a basic human need. According to research into adults and play, play time can be an important means of reducing stress and supporting overall well-being. Play can relieve stress.[8] It has been found highly playful young adults reported less stress in their lives and possessed better coping skills. Play boosts creativity, improves brain function, and improves our relationships with other people. In workplaces, play has been found to speed up learning, enhance productivity and increase job satisfaction. Play allows individuals and groups to explore creativity and find different and unique solutions.

Taking time out to play together at home strengthens relationships and communication. Giving yourself permission to be more playful leads to a whole list of benefits; mental, emotional and physical. [9, 10]

"Honestly, I feel like I have been re-born."

Grandmother post laughter play session

"What all play has in common is that it offers a sense of engagement and pleasure, takes the player out of a sense of time and place, and the experience of doing it is more important than the outcome."

Stuart Brown [11]

Exercise: Self-reflection break

- What types of play did you enjoy as a child?
- How much do you play now and how do you play?
- How can you connect the play when you were a child to where you are in life now?

Why laughter play?

For many generations, play was unstructured: child-led, open-ended activity with little direction by adults. [12] This type of free play led to children creating their own happiness, develop self-reliance and self-esteem. It provided a cultivation of creativity and imagination. As adults, all of these skills can be harnessed with laughter play, which generates play on your own terms as opposed to adult play activities such as sports and clubs, etc., with an overemphasis on rules and structure. Laughter play can be individual, a sole activity and enhance inventiveness. The focus is on the actual experience and not on accomplishing a goal. The ease about laughter play is that it can take place alongside other activities. We can be free to choose and bring playfulness and lightness during the day, without another adult's intervention. Laughter play can take seconds and minutes and, once harnessed regularly, is at the forefront to be accessed easily for immersion and relief. The structure of daily life can be joyfully infused with space for natural play. Laughter is play, with movement, pleasure and peace to strength the mind, body, and enjoy release.

"The laughter play exercise helps me let go and not think about anything except for the fun I am having in that moment. Those few minutes really do help."

Carer, aged 55

How to laughter play

A little bit of laughter play can boost your happiness and creativity. What can happen if you generate playful laughter? We don't need to play every second of the day to enjoy play's benefits, but regular bouts of playful laughter, on your own, can boost your productivity and happiness. Here are some laughter play exercises...

1. Laughter play combined with other activities

Think of the things you do on a daily basis and use them as a cue to laugh regularly. Here are what some of my clients have shared:

- I now remember to laugh every time I tie my shoelaces.
- I laugh lots in the shower. My private space and the water flow makes my laugh sound more amazing.
- I laugh when I enter my home. It's like I am infusing me and our house with positivity. I placed a laughing Buddha statue to remind me. I laugh with him too!
- I laugh every time I open the refrigerator (I have a note reminding me). I laugh even more when I take dessert out!
- I have put a sign on the TV saying 'laugh'. I laugh before I put the news on and after. It balances out the negativity.
- I end my meditation with gratitude and now have added a giggle too. It helps me focus back into the present and energise me. Sometimes I can laugh for a long time and sometimes its short. I go with what happens.
- Once I have dropped my daughter off, I get in the car and give a big cheer and laugh. I love my daughter but I relish my own short free time in the car and it's great. I explained what you said to another mum and she does the same too!

- When I hear the phone ringing, I smile and as much as possible, laugh before I answer.
- I laugh when I wash the pots. My teenage son thinks I am crazy but he said he is happy to see me laughing instead of yelling.

2. Laughter play with movement

When you're laughing, everything is moving inside, breath is deepened and even the internal organs are moving. Laughter causes the tissue in the inner lining of blood vessels to expand allowing more blood flow. Movement can cause immediate stress reduction. So adding laughter with external movement can be a multi-tasking approach to maximising health in a fun way. Others have said:

- I have added laughing to the end of my morning stretching routine. It feels like I am stretching more parts of me and is so easy to do.
- When I circuit walk in my garden, I add laughter to my steps. have started alternating with 'ha-ha-ha' and 'ho-ho-ho'. The dog stares at me and then I laugh even more. My wife is happy that I am looking less frowny!
- I remembered you shared that smiling before weightlifting can help. It makes me feel better, more confident and more energised. It does work... I told my trainer and he was amazed.
- I am still housebound but walking down the stairs and around the house laughing cheers me up, I feel I am doing more and getting stronger.
- Pushing my baby's buggy and laughing made me feel better.
- As a cleaner, laughing when I do the worst jobs certainly helps.
- I stood behind a chair and laughed and swayed as you

showed me in the class. Moving like that felt freeing and surprisingly relaxing. When I remember, I hold the back of the kitchen chair and sway and laugh before I cook… it helps me feel less stressed about cooking the family meal.

- When I am feeling down, I clap my hands and sometimes smile and sometimes laugh. Sometimes, I only clap quietly and whisper a laugh but I still do it.

Laughter play using a mirror

For many of us, looking in the mirror can bring up self-judgements. But if you persist, you will begin to see through those judgements and see who you really are. This process can be made easier with laughter play. Each time you do these mirror exercises, it tends to feel a little less awkward and more comfortable and you gain more confidence and creativity. Find alone time when you won't be disturbed so you can let go completely.

Here are some of the creative laughter play you can explore with a mirror.

- Wink and laugh at yourself in the mirror. Explore different types of winking (e.g. alternative eye winking or winking from a side pose). Watch what emerges. It may just be a smile initially or surprisingly a loud laugh. Perhaps you can wink and smile at yourself each time you pass a mirror (I do).
- Hide your face in your hands and play peek-a-boo and laugh. It can help you access your inner child and draw out your playfulness in a big way.
- Pretend you are an actor and need to laugh for a part you are playing. Perhaps you have a serious role. Look in the mirror and laugh in a serious manner! Exaggerate

your laughter. The role has changed and now you are a pantomime character. Can you laugh to match the role? Think of your favourite character on TV or in a film, how do they laugh or how would you imagine they would laugh? Explore laughing in different ways.

- Smile at the person in the mirror and say out loud 'Thank you' as you receive your own smile back. Follow with a laugh and say a 'Thank you' as you laugh with the person in the mirror... you. Repeat as many times as you can. How do you feel?

Approach laughter play in a relaxed way

Have you experienced the following: the more you care about the outcome, the harder it feels to achieve? Sometimes, when we decide we are going to do an amazing job on our new goal and we get serious, we can burden ourselves with high expectations, procrastinate (delay) and perhaps put off the task and even add more pressure on ourselves. However, if we approach the task in a more light-hearted way, we can start and achieve what we set out to do. Sometimes, the less you care, the more naturally it comes to you. Rather than making a plan to laugh loads and loads (especially if you are not used to doing this), choose to laugh a little bit more. Treat it as a game, be gentle on yourself. Little but often is key and daily is better.

Why action matters

"It isn't confidence that comes first, but taking action. Confidence follows action."

Scott Allan

For a while, I thought I needed to get confidence and motivation first and then I could take action. Once I was inspired, I would have the positive mindset and a stronger will to achieve my goals and win at life. It happened, I took steps but it was short-lived, and exploring it I realised it was because of my changing emotions. The highs and lows of the emotional landscape is not always easy to control. The self-discipline was there to complete goals for employers and clients, but for my own laid out plans, it was a different matter.

Once I stumbled upon a simple strategy, I was on the path of achieving just about anything including laughing more and finishing this book! The winning game plan was to take action, however small towards the goal I had set. Each movement towards a plan created the confidence and motivation to continue forwards. If I had a slight affinity not to do an action step, I would move... move my arms, legs or shake my body. Movement took me away from negative thoughts and steered me into taking action towards my goal.

Once you take action, it is easier to stay in motion, but the most difficult part is getting going, the very first action. Have you ever helped to push a stationary car into moving? Once that initial effort is applied, the car moves so much more easily. Similarly, your actions will gather momentum, and success aids and expands motivation onto goal completion. A client once asked, how do I know laughter is for me and will help me? I responded, "Start to walk on your path to laugh more, then you can assess if you have taken the correct route."

The learning journey

"Change is the end result of all true learning."

Leo Buscaglia

Learning is a natural response to encountering something new. I share the following with my clients to help them adapt to the laugh-more journey.

The learning quest can be thought of as having five levels. They are **Awareness, Awkwardness, Application, Assimilation** and finally **Art**. Learning about the benefits of laughter provides awareness. You gain knowledge; then as you become 'aware' of something else related to what you know, that adds to your knowledge. Understanding arises and so can appreciation. Laughing more initially might feel awkward but when you indulge more laughter practice, you eventually get past awkwardness and get into the application of laughing more frequently and with ease.

By repeating this process frequently, you will be in the zone and you will arrive at the assimilation and easily digest the techniques of laughing frequently and easily. Laughter fits into your life.

"Assimilation for me meant that the laughter got bigger and bigger in my life, like a balloon filling up. I saw laughter opportunities everywhere and I could fit it in easily and add even more, even with my clients."

Solicitor

Laughter can become an art form. You could even add your own artistic touch like I did, creating laughter courses, volunteering with community groups and laughing professionally!

Exercise: Self-reflection break

- What's one thing that I could do today that would make me laugh?
- Can I set a laughter play plan? What would it look like?

Get your grit!

"As much as talent counts, effort counts twice."

Angela Duckworth [13]

Did I have a natural talent for laughing lots? No. I grew up in a culture where it could be frowned upon to laugh loudly and I do remember on a few occasions being told off by my father, for being loud in my giggles. I certainly smiled a lot, but my smiles were not always genuine smiles. But once I chose to laugh more, I practised and I practised with passion, putting in continuous efforts. I used grit.

Charles Portis was the author of the western *True Grit* (1968), which was turned into a 1969 film starring John Wayne (one of my father's favourite films). Wayne's character is hired to bring in a killer, because he had 'true grit'. 'Grit' is small pieces of stone and sand, hard and unyielding and when you transfer that quality to a person's character, you have 'true grit'... fortitude, determination and courage. It also includes the commitment to finish what you start, to rise from setbacks, to want to improve and succeed, and to undertake sustained practice and overcome obstacles.

Apply true grit to your laugh more journey... carry on, to continue, and head to the next chapter, where we learn the one thing that makes you 30 times more likely to laugh.

"...your actions will gather momentum, and success aids and expands motivation onto goal completion"

Sam Rehan

CHAPTER 6
LAUGHING WITH OTHERS

"Laughter is the shortest distance between two people."

Victor Borge

Arthur was unable to talk but attended a group laughter session I facilitated for those living with dementia or memory/cognition issues. To his surprise, he could make laughter sounds alongside the other attendees. He was giddy with glee and my heart melted to see his beaming smile. I was running late, but Arthur make gestures that he wanted to write something on the feedback form. I waited with patience, as he carefully took 30 minutes to formulate five words. He wrote, "Thank you for my laugh." (To this day, that is still one of my favourite memories of laughing with another human.)

We rarely laugh when we are alone. You may laugh because you heard a good joke, but it's more often likely your laughter was caused by another person. Most laughter is not about humour; it is about relationships between people and we use humour and laughter to form and maintain relationships. We laugh a lot when talking to friends, mostly about statements and comments. Most people find that they remain nearly silent, even during a funny movie or comedy show, enjoying the humour internally. It's when we spend time with others that we laugh out loud, with genuine amusement and the resulting moments of shared joy. The main trigger for laughter is another person. [1]

Laughter is a language that we all speak and it binds

people together. We feel safe and connected to the people we are laughing with. Laughter is about the relationship between people and is contagious.

"Laughter is a social glue that bonds people together who are members of your group, this is kind of an ancient biological way of drawing us together. We don't will it to happen. It just happens."

Robert Provine

The frequency of laughter

It is reported that adults tend to laugh some 17 times a day on average and much of this laughter is with others. [2] You are 30 times more likely to laugh if there's somebody else with you than if you're on your own.[3] Laughter occurs when people are comfortable with one another and more laughter leads to more bonding. This feedback 'loop' of bonding-laughter-more bonding, combined with the common desire to be part of a social group, may be another reason why laughter is often contagious.

See if you can laugh right now. It is difficult to laugh on command. Laughter often occurs without us thinking about it and is triggered by many sensations and thoughts. The most laughs take place in a social setting where there is playfulness, group safety and positive emotions.

Children laugh substantially more times than adults and researchers looking at the adult/child laugh ratio gap wondered why children laugh so much more. [4] They found the answer lies in the number of interactions. Looking at mother/infant ratios, rates of laughter were almost equal because of the high level of interaction. [5] Time with children increases laughter. It seems that the frequency of laughter for all ages is dependent on how much time people spend together. We can increase our laughter by increasing our connections and spending more time in the company of children.

Sweetening

In television, sweetening refers to the use of a laugh track in addition to a live studio audience. The laugh track adds laughter sound effects and 'enhances' the laughter for television audiences, sometimes in cases where a joke or scene intended to be funny does not draw the expected response, and sometimes to avoid awkward sound edits when a scene is shortened or more than one take is used in editing. Laugh tracks also originated as a way to engage an at-home audience into a more-traditional, social, theatre-like experience, so viewers feel like they are in a room full of laughing happy people. [6]

In 1953, a machine for producing fake 'canned' laughter, accessible at the push of a button or pull of a lever, was created. Some shows used the canned laughter technique very obviously rather than the 'in-between' laugh-track technique. An obvious sign of this is that the laughter is more or less identical in volume or magnitude, regardless of the scene. How does canned laughter affect the 'funny' rating?

A professional comedian recorded jokes and two versions were created, one with staged, canned laughter and the second with real, spontaneous laughter. In the research study all of the jokes were heard with both different kinds of laughter. The findings were that the addition of any type of laughter improved the 'funny' rating of the jokes – even the bad ones. But everyone in the study found jokes funniest when paired with spontaneous laughter. The findings also suggest laughter might be contagious or give others permission to also laugh. "This research shows that while canned laughter does elevate the humour of a comedy, adding real laughter would get a better response." Sophie Scott [7]

What is your play style?

Social rules and cultural factors may impact expressions of playfulness in a society. [8] Not all adults play alike and this has been explored, and four different types of playful adults has been described. [9]

- **Other-directed** – people who like to fool around with friends, colleagues, relatives and acquaintances.
- **Light-hearted** – people regard their whole life as a type of game and are not preoccupied by the future consequences of their behaviour.
- **Intellectual** – those who like to play with thoughts and ideas and are able to turn monotonous tasks into something interesting.
- **Whimsical** – tend to be interested in strange and unusual things and are amused by small everyday observations.

Your 'play style' can give you information and encourage you to be more playfully engaged with others for opportunities of more laughter and bonding. A less playful person can learn to be more playful. There is a positive relationship between being playful and the experience of positive emotions. Playful people are said to be able to reinterpret situations in their lives so that they experience them as entertaining and this can aid well-being. [10]

Exercise: Self-reflection break

- Which of the four playful styles do you identify with?
- How can you use this information to engage with others for more opportunities for fun?

- What other play styles do you recognise in members of your social group; family, friends and co-workers?

How to make laughter happen more easily

Laughter is 30 times more likely to happen in social settings, where we can bond and connect. Ideally aim to laugh together for at least 15 minutes today as this period of time, alongside hearty belly laughs, help you to access the full health benefits. [11]

Rules around laughter... anything that makes anyone uncomfortable must be excluded and this includes both physical touching and verbal communication.

Here are some ways to engage with laughter and generate more:

- Laughter is a great subject matter to bring up with loved ones. Ask your friends and family what makes them laugh. Share stories and experiences where laughter and humour took place.
- Select to spend time with friends who are playful.
- Become aware of your play style (described earlier in this chapter) and use this information to become more playfully engaged with others.
- Spend time with children. Playing with kids helps us experience the magic of play through their perspective and share in their natural laughter.
- Attend a laughter yoga session. These sessions use playful group exercises to generate and lengthen laughter. Speak to the facilitator to find out how the session is run and check the instructor is qualified. My sessions are without yoga positions (yoga refers to the healthy breathing that arises from hearty laughter) and laughter is invited without the use of fake laughter.

- If you are isolated, ring a friend or tell a carer you want to laugh more. Perhaps share what is the funniest thing that happened to you both recently. Locate an online laughter club to engage in group laughter; many do not require you to be on video.

"I did what you recommend. I went through my photo albums and created a laughter album of all my favourite people smiling. When I can, I will add to it."

Sally, Housebound

Exercise: Self-reflection break

- Do I laugh enough with other people?
- With who can I create opportunities to laugh more with?

Fake laughter

How much fake laughter can we detect? Researchers found that people mistake fake for genuine laughter a third of the time,[12] which is probably a low estimate as the results did not arise from natural social situations. Genuine laughter is generated differently by the body compared to volitional laughter (done deliberately). A fake laugh is reported to have speech sounds in it as it is produced more from areas used for speech. [13]

"People half-heartedly chuckle throughout most casual conversations, regardless of the topic. It's a modern extension of the verbalized pause, built by TV laugh tracks. Everyone in America has three laughs: a real laugh, a fake real laugh, and a 'filler laugh' they use during impersonal conversations. We have been trained to connect conversation with soft, interstitial laughter. It's our way of showing the other person that we understand the context of the interaction, even when we don't."

Chuck Klosterman

Fake laughter – caution

"Laughter is so expected and part of the social norm that when we don't laugh, it's a really powerful message."

Eden King [14]

Social conventions are rules and norms governing the many behaviours all of us engage in every day without necessarily thinking about them, from shaking hands to laughing. Should we laugh to fit in or follow our instincts and be authentic?

Polite laughter can be heard in conversation, at parties and at work. A fake or uneasy laugh is often used to acknowledge, approve and show generosity. In many circumstances this may be kind, but it's damaging in situations where people are being inappropriate, offensive and hurtful and discredits you if you routinely laugh when you don't mean it. Do you give a hollow laugh and move on? What if something that was said was unkind and is not confronted? I think most of us pick up when something is inappropriate. Feigned laughter is one way to brush off uncomfortable situations. Sometimes nervous laughter arises as a form of protection for what is being said or done.

I propose to increase the trend for not laughing at the 'joke' and facing the possible discomfort you may cause when you say 'that's not funny'. Psychoanalyst Dr Jane Yates, recommends, instead of laughing, filling the dead air following an unwanted or inept comment with something neutral like, 'Well, then', or maybe just, 'Hmmm'. But she adds that takes a good bit of self-awareness to pull off. [15] Personally, I have used the phrase 'Moving on'.

Disparagement humour

Disparagement humour is any attempt to amuse through the denigration (put-down, vilify) of a social group or its representatives. For example, sexist or racist jokes or any that makes a punchline out of a marginalised group. Disparagement humour communicates two conflicting messages. One is a hostile or prejudiced message and alongside is a second message that it's not prejudiced because 'it's just a joke'.

When it comes to humour that belittles an individual or social group, research indicates that even though disparagements are framed as a joke, repeated exposure to such humour can cause us to take situations, such as racism or sexism, less seriously and can foster discrimination against targeted groups. There are social norms about acceptable and unacceptable humour, which allow disparagement humour to flourish. Perhaps as individuals we can stop, pause and respond to widen acceptable behaviour so it contains less and less disparagement humour. [16, 17]

People should not be afraid to say something for fear that they will offend, if it's coming from a genuine and honest place. I'd like to see humour continue to evolve, so it is full of more kindness.

Not feeling the laughter

What if you are with a group of people and they are laughing and you aren't? When most other people are laughing, we can wonder if something is wrong with us. It's a natural feeling; we are social animals and have a built in need to fit in and be welcome in groups. [18]

Here are what some clients have shared:

"It wasn't my kind of humour, and I just observed and then the conversation passed to something I could join in with."

"Humour is much like beauty. What one person (or even many people) finds beautiful, another may not. If I don't feel like laughing, I don't."

"I can be quiet and shy. Friends sometimes roar with laughter and I don't always get why they are laughing. I guess I smile and join in when I can.

Luckily they get me and I don't get stressed by it."

"Many people laugh at things that are not funny. I find most things funny and laugh; if I don't, I smile but I don't pretend to laugh. The smile helps me feel I am still part of it."

"I am lucky I can be with people who bring out my laughter and smiles. If I don't laugh and smile (more to do with what's going on with me), I don't feel pressured by them and that I am grateful for."

"I think I laugh a lot less than my friends. They cheer me up even though I might not show it outwardly. Just the way I am."

"I tend to laugh more with people who I know really well. I am guarded when I am with people who I know less well and I laugh less with them. I think that is normal, yes?"

Perhaps you are with friends or family or even at a yoga laughter club. Some people have shared with me that they attended other laughter yoga classes where they felt they were forced to laugh by being asked to fake laugh and pretend. Some shared that they felt bad and others shared that some laughter emerged.

At the end of the day, we want nothing more in life than to be ourselves... and that is feeling authenticity. Vulnerability is being our authentic selves with another person and it feels real. In my opinion and experience, being forced to laugh does not feel good. Naturally arisen laughter feels good. In my laughter sessions, I always have some chairs at the side. I share that I invite laughter and don't enforce it. People can get up at any time and choose to exit the exercise, without any reason. In my work, it is 100% OK not to share and opt out. I say, "Thank you for sharing how you feel right now." The beauty is that often if we can't laugh, we smile and if we can't smile, we can soften.

Part two of this book, describes challenges of laughter and where you can locate support.

The gift of laughter

Giving to others is wonderful, it offers kindness, empathy and support and when you give to others it can have a direct positive effect on your own mental well-being. [19]

We all have something to offer... have you considered that striking up a conversation, smiling and sharing your humour with laughter may be a small act of kindness towards other people, but that the gift for the other can be huge? Seeing yourself, spreading happiness, linked to the wider community can be incredibly rewarding and creates connections with the people around you. Lifting somebody up with a bout of laughter can mean that they are more likely to extend positivity to others in a way that may not have happened.

Feelings of happiness are strongly linked with active participation in social and community life. Sharing your smiles and stopping to engage with a light conversation is linked with an increased sense of self-worth and positive feelings. Individuals who report a greater interest in helping others are more likely to rate themselves as happy. [20]

"Whenever you make someone laugh or smile you are doing the world a great service. This is especially true for strangers, the natural distance between yourself and a stranger is always shortened through laughter. When you make others laugh it feels good to see the positivity emerge in the other. You are connected in a deep way, if only for seconds. The more laughter and positivity there is in the world, the better off humanity as a whole will be."

Retired teacher

Connect with others and laugh if you can.

In the next chapter, you can learn how to make laughter a habit so you can feel more connected each day.

"At the end of the day, we want nothing more in life than to be ourselves... and that is feeling authenticity."

Sam Rehan

CHAPTER 7
MAKING LAUGHTER A DAILY HABIT

"If you pick the right small behaviour and sequence it right, then you won't have to motivate yourself to have it grow. It will just happen naturally, like a good seed planted in a good spot."

B. J. Fogg

"I did as you shared! I put little gold sticker stars around the house; at the side of a mirror, in the kitchen, and even the bathroom. When I glance at the stars, it's been a great reminder for me to have a little laugh. I am laughing more and it feels good. I have told my friends. Thank you for helping me laugh more; I needed it."

Senior

Your life is essentially behaviours and actions you undertake each day. What do you do every day without thinking about too much, for example cleaning your teeth in the morning and perhaps ending the day with a shower. You do not have set alerts to remind you to do them, as these are actions have become habits.

A habit is created by our brains. Habits are behaviours which are performed automatically because they have been performed frequently in the past. When habits emerge, the brain stops fully participating in decision making. By creating habits, it clears its workload and has more brain power for tasks that require more effort than brushing your teeth. Having habits means some actions don't have to be done consciously and it's less exhausting for your brain. Habits are the main reason why some people thrive more than others, even if their backgrounds were challenging. Your habits determine success. It stands to reason that since you learned every habit you have, you can also learn new ones. [1]

DID YOU KNOW? Over 40% of what we do is determined not by decisions but by habits. This suggests that we can change a huge part of our lives by creating good habits. [2]

If you embark on any form of change, you gain stability and comfort though practising something daily. Your habits may be small, such as smiling more or adding extra laughter into your day, but they can have a considerable impact on your health and even your relationships, as regular action cements and magnifies them. An action that is a positive habit is a very powerful addition to your life. Daily practice of good habits extends your comfort zone and boosts productivity. Positive habits add up.

"The man who spends all his time on his own needs, who organises every day as though it were his last, neither longs for nor fears the next day."
Seneca

How to adopt a habit in three steps

I found it easier to adopt new good habits once I understood how habits are formed in the first place. [3, 4, 5]

Every habit has three parts:

The cue – This is the trigger that prompts and reminds you to carry out your habit. Our brain responds to it automatically. The cue can be emotional, for example wanting to have a break from your desk and getting up to chat to a co-worker, time of day (e.g. checking the time and it is your normal time to go to bed), sight (e.g. seeing your plate empty and taking and putting it next to the sink), location (e.g. walking past your favourite cafe and purchasing a drink) and another person (e.g. bumping into someone you know and shaking their hand).

A routine – This is the action you carry out, for example putting your plate next to the sink, purchasing a drink and shaking someone's hand.

A reward – This is what you get and is the reason you are guided by the cue and routine in the first place. For example, shaking hands with a friend feels good. Taking your plate to the sink feels good, you are contributing and avoiding arguments. Having your favourite drink feels wonderful and comforting. If the reward is positive, your brain will remember the habit and want to repeat it. When a habit is repeated over and over again and consistently delivers a positive reward, the brain develops a longing for it. The longing can be considered as energy for the habit, making the routine become more and more automatic and helps the habit to stick in the long term.

Craft your smile and laughter habit

"When one good habit triggers another, the speed of success doubles."

Tyler Tervooren

Smiling is something simple (for most of us) that we can cultivate as a daily habit and add laughter too.

You can use the three parts to craft a new habit of smiling and laughing more. If we choose to establish a smile and laughter habit, it becomes easier to laugh more and live a life of more laughter.

The routine is to laugh and smile more, for example, to smile for at least 30 seconds and build up to a minute. The laughter can be a short chuckle, a quiet laugh or a playful loud laugh. The reward can be feeling emotionally happier and more relaxed after smiling and laughing. The reward can be to treat yourself, for example to a massage or a meal with a friend if you can smile and laugh at least three times a day for a whole month. How will you trigger your habit (the cue)? You can set an alarm on your phone or place a sign/sticker near a mirror you view frequently, or choose to laugh and smile upon waking or getting ready for bed.

If you don't normally laugh and smile a lot, you may need support to continue the habit, because you haven't yet experienced a reward worth craving. Perhaps a reward after day 7, then day 14. Or set it up so the reward is straight after the routine of smiling and laughing, such as a cup of coffee or call to a friend. To really experience these rewards, it is important for you to tune in to them: being mindful, relaxed and open to simple pleasures. The mere feeling of smiling and laughing can become intensely rewarding in itself. Smiling may seem a small, seemingly insignificant action, but it can lead to reaping huge positive rewards from being practised every day.

"Success is nothing more than a few simple disciplines, practiced every day."

Jim Rohn

Exercise: Create a laughter habit

Create a smile and laughter habit using the three steps outlined above. Write it down to further cement it and place it in a visible place to look at regularly.

For example, here is my own regular laughter habit: when I drop my child to school, I will laugh in the car for a minute or so, in order to gain relaxation for completing the morning school routine. Another one of mine: when I wake up in the middle of night, I will smile and visualise a happy event in order to gain relaxation to help me to fall back to sleep.

DID YOU KNOW? It takes an average 66 days to form a new habit. Research shows that missing one opportunity did not significantly impact the habit formation process, but people who were very inconsistent in performing the behaviour did not succeed in making habits. There was considerable variation in the number of days to form a new habit... ranging from 18 to 254 days.[6]

How to significantly increase your chance of achieving your goal

One way you can increase your chance of achieving your goal is by writing them down. **It has been found that you are 42% more likely to achieve your goals and dreams, simply by writing them down on a regular basis. This helps the process of thinking about your goal and begin taking action towards it. Goals that are written are more likely to be achieved.**[7]

Supercharge yourself with a 60-second smile

"You'll never change your life until you change something you do daily. The secret of your success is found in your daily routine."

John C. Maxwell

My life changed enormously when I began to do certain habits each morning. Many, if not all, successful people attribute their daily habits to their success.

I will share one daily habit with you now that I use to generate positivity and calm before the day begins. Small daily actions lead to big results and one such action is smiling. There are 86,400 seconds in a day. You can create a habit to smile, for 60 of those seconds... Every morning, upon awakening, I access joy by feeling grateful for being alive another day, another day I can breathe and experience life and be with family and friends. The gratefulness allows me to access a genuine smile and I smile for a minute or so, thinking happy thoughts. I am pretty sure this one habit feeds and propels my positivity and success for the day ahead.

Habit stacking

Habit stacking is a great method to create new habits faster and build a routine of tasks that benefit you that stick. We can use a habit to trigger another habit, each habit take place, because the beginning of one is triggered by the end of another. For example, here is my morning routine: when I first open my eyes that is a cue for me to say a small prayer of gratitude that I am alive for another day. The habit of feeling gratitude is a cue for me to smile for a minute or so (my 60-second smile). Getting out bed, I choose to put on my workout clothes, and that's my cue for my habit to stretch. At the end of my stretch, is a trigger for my habit to sway and laugh for a minute.

Here is how you can create a morning routine with smiling. First, let's choose the habit of smiling for 60 seconds in the morning. Next, specify which habit you're going to use as a trigger for your new habit. Link the new habit with a current habit. For example, after I wake up, I will smile for 60 seconds, or after I have brushed my teeth I will smile for 60 seconds while I look in the mirror. Experiment to see what works for YOU. To help you establish the habit, write down your habit stack and put it somewhere you'll see every morning so you can commit and follow.

My morning routine developed as I chose to change one thing at a time, I did simple things and I made the habits automatic by practising them every day. I now have a string of habits which include smiling and laughing.

Snigger trigger[8]

A trigger is an event that will kick off that automatic urge to do a habit and it works best to find a trigger that's already part of your daily routine. A trigger snigger is coined by me to remind you to activate your habit of laughing and smiling, when you take certain action. Habits become automatic after we've created a bond between the trigger and the habit — the stronger the bond, the more ingrained the habit and repetition is key!

For example, some of my snigger trigger are phones, my home and my car.

When the phone rings, I get in a positive mind state, smile and then answer. I do the same when I make calls.

When I walk into my home, it is a trigger for me to snigger (laugh).

When I enter or exit my car, I chuckle.

What I love about my snigger triggers is that where, previously, I used to do things such as entering my home automatically or answering the phone without a thought, I am now more present, alert and in the moment. Now, in recurring actions, I have mindfulness moments.

Exercise: What trigger(s) work for you

Find triggers that happen regularly and link them with smiling and/or laughing. Some examples of triggers: waking up, brushing your teeth, showering, putting clothes on, eating breakfast, feeding pets, checking email/social media, taking the kids to school, driving, etc.

Exercise: Habit stack a morning smile

Choose your habit to smile for at least 60 seconds each morning. Remember to visualise happy memories for a genuine smile, by thinking of all the good in your life. If that is difficult, remember a positive memory, or imagine the sun shining down and beaming support to you. Choose your cue. The most reliable cues are immediately preceding actions/

behaviours you already do. For example, after I wake up, I will smile for 60 seconds, or before (or after) I brush my teeth, I will smile for 60 seconds. To experience the reward, tune in to the relaxed, happy feelings generated in you, from smiling for 60 seconds. Name those feelings internally or externally; is it peace, joy, contentment, gratitude, presence or other feelings and emotions? To help you establish this new habit, write down your habit stack and put it somewhere you'll see every morning so you can commit, follow and establish as a daily habit.

Post reminders of your new habit choices to support you. Every single day, commit to doing your new habit right after the trigger, immediately. Firm focus and a willingness will reap the rewards.

"Habit is a cable; we weave a thread each day, and at last we cannot break it."

Horace Mann

Exercise: Tell and talk to a friend

Discussing your goal to smile and laugh more is very effective when you say it out loud and tell another person other than yourself. As you continue your goal and update your friend, it feels rewarding and will motivate you to do it again and stay committed and generate positive emotions. Additionally, you are likely to inspire your friend and get the smiling habit acquired by more people!

DID YOU KNOW? It has also been found that, more than 70% of the participants who sent weekly updates to a friend reported successful goal achievement (completely accomplished their goal or were more than half way there), compared to 35% of those who kept their goals to themselves, without writing them down. [9]

Establish a streak

"If you can't measure it, you can't improve it."

Peter Drucker

If you're serious about habit forming, you need to track your progress. When you track, you can evaluate and adjust your progress to reach your goals. When you track, you can see how far you've come or what adjustments and support are needed to make progress. Daily progress tracking is key so you know what you are doing is working. If you measure something, you know the results, and you can confirm if you are getting better... no measurement, no idea! Here is a visual way to measure if you are succeeding in smiling and laughing more.

A streak is just a visual reminder of how many consecutive times you have achieved something. Perhaps many of us experienced this when we created a chart for our children as a visual reminder for teeth brushing. In games, it's often used to track wins but you can also use it to track when you have a boost of laughter and smiling. The easiest way to do this is to take a calendar and put an X in the box every time you do something to generate more laughter. Soon enough, you'll have a neat row of Xs there to show off as your streak.

Welcome wariness from others

You may hear others wary, critical and suspicious when you habit form. They may remind you that you have failed before or that it's silly. This could even be the case when they see a bit of success, as it can remind them of their own journey. If you struggle and it's taking longer, they can call you out on it, telling you that you should have never tried to achieve that goal in the first place. Their spoken thoughts might mirror what you are thinking too and add to the struggle. I welcome that criticism and allow it to energise me to achieve my goals rather than to hold me back. Change is hard and can be viewed as stressful and remind others that perhaps they are not succeeding, learning and moving forwards. Check in with yourself and reflect: why do you want to establish change and create this new positive habit? If you want something bad enough and it is important enough, then you will push ahead no matter what anyone has to say about it. Share your journey, enlist friends who support you and cheer you on every step of the way. Upwards and onwards.

The key: maintaining momentum

"If you are interested, you'll do what's convenient. If you're committed, you'll do whatever it takes."

John Assaraf

As we practise things, even though it feels like we are making no progress at all, we are taking action and turning new behaviours into habits. Learning is happening all along. The hardest part about building positive habits is sticking to them long enough so they stick and you do them automatically and THIS IS HARD. To make new, positive habits, you have to stay with them even when you experience failure (an almost certainty). Learn to welcome failure as it's all part of the learning and every success story contains failure. First accept it. Understand why it happened. What can you learn from it? Take action to continue and the key step is not to avoid failure all together but plan for it. Remind yourself why you choose the habit and why it's meaningful to you and if you want to be doing it. If you do, you will find a way to continue to succeed. On some days, I can only manage seconds of smiling or laughing but it means I am still sticking to my schedule even for a very short bit... but I keep the momentum going. People are surprised when I share I can't always smile easily.

"Failure is simply the opportunity to begin again, this time more intelligently."

Henry Ford

Intelligence, in my experience, means more sticky notes reminders, tracking and taking action without unhelpful thoughts side tracking us ('I will do it later', or 'one day missed is okay' or 'I will do extra tomorrow'). If you miss a couple, just acknowledging that you're going in the right direction makes your brain give you a burst of positivity to keep on going.

Daily laughter with gratitude

What is gratitude?

"Gratitude helps you to grow and expand; gratitude brings joy and laughter into your life and into the lives of all those around you."

Eileen Caddy

Gratitude, derived from the Latin word *gratia,* means gratefulness or thankfulness. Positive psychology, the scientific study of the strengths that enable individuals and communities to thrive, describes gratitude as the human way of acknowledging the good things of life. Difficulties, hardships and burdens are not ignored. If we choose to look at life as a whole, gratitude encourages us to identify the good things in our life, however small. For example, moments in life which generate laughter and help us feel happy and joyful. Gratitude has been described as a positive emotional response that we perceive on giving or receiving a benefit from someone. [10]

Gratitude can be thought of as having two components.[11] Firstly, it's acknowledging the good things and the second part of gratitude is recognising where the goodness comes from. For example, we can be thankful for the positive traits in ourselves, and other people and higher powers. If we hear laughter from others or catch a smile from a neighbour or passer-by, we can be grateful for those who have contributed to the positivity that can pass to us.

Gratitude generates better health

"At times, our own light goes out and is rekindled by a spark from another person. Each of us has cause to think with deep gratitude of those who have lighted the flame within us."

Albert Schweitzer

Your brain cannot simultaneously focus on positive and negative things at once. Because of this, practising gratitude can help you shift your focus from being sad about the things you don't have in your life to being glad for the things you do have. Researchers say gratitude is a big contributor to happiness in life, suggesting that the more we cultivate gratitude, the happier we will be. Gratitude in any form can make us feel happier, have a healing effect on and illuminates positive feelings. Scientific studies reveal gratitude is good for our bodies, our minds and our relationships. When you engage in the act of being thankful for something, we produce feel-good chemicals and this activates the happiness centre of the brain. This is similar to how antidepressants work; so, you could think of gratitude as a natural antidepressant. [12] Gratitude magnifies positive emotions like those linked with laughter and makes us appreciate the value of something. When we appreciate the value of laughter, we can gain more from it and are less likely to take it for granted. Within a week or so, many people experience a boost in well-being along with an increase in gratitude for many other things.

DID YOU KNOW? Research has shown that writing in a gratitude journal improves sleep. In short, when you cultivate gratitude throughout the day, you're more likely to have positive thoughts as you're drifting off to sleep. [13]

Exercise: Laughter gratitude journal

A gratitude journal offers a method of identifying and reflecting on all of the good things in your life – all the things you can choose to be grateful for. I invite you to write down three things you are grateful for each day, which made you LAUGH or SMILE or both! A gratitude list is more effective if you make them more specific, about the gratitude and where the gratitude came from. For example, instead of writing 'My sister', it is more effective to expand and write 'I'm grateful for my sister for making me burst into laughter when we were talking in the garden.' The expanded writing creates a deeper sensation of gratitude in us.

"Thank you for sharing your laughter gratitude journal exercise with me. I kept mine in the kitchen and despite long days with the children and a husband who works long hours, I managed to scribble down thanks for my laughter. I realised I laughed more than I thought I did, mostly at the TV, but I do laugh and I am starting to laugh more. You'll be happy to know I am finding more ways to laugh, I have my children helping me – they ask me to read my laughter diary to them. And do you know, I am finding more than laughter to be grateful for. It's great. Those few minutes of writing, I look forward to."

Mum of three

Here are some more wonderful ways to remind yourself to laugh daily:

- Purchase some small dots or star stickers. Affix them in places you regularly frequent. For example, I have shiny stars attached to my bathroom mirror and my car dashboard. They are great reminders for me to smile, chortle and laugh out loud, each time the stickers catch my eye.
- Laughing when doing daily chores we don't particularly enjoy is another way to generate more happiness and

health. Some people aim to laugh in regular places; one senior shared that he remembered to laugh every time he tied his shoelaces, another reported they laughed regularly in the bathroom, garage or garden. My daily laughter practice takes place in the car after the school run.

- Is there someone you call every day? Share with them your new healthy habit of laughing more. Much like a running partner, can they be your laughter buddy and laughter support?

"Rewards will always come to someone who commits to the practice, but the rewards are not the goal. The practice is the goal. Perhaps we'll never know how far the path can go, how much a human being can truly achieve, until we realise that the ultimate reward is not a gold medal but the path itself."

George Leonard

Enjoy building your habit of adding laughter and smiles to your life and enjoy where it takes you.

Onwards to the next chapter where we explore laughter in the workplace.

"Gratitude magnifies positive emotions like those linked with laughter and makes us appreciate the value of something."

Sam Rehan

CHAPTER 8
LAUGHTER, WORKPLACE PERFORMANCE AND MORE

"If you can laugh together, you can work together."

Robert Orben

Smiling and laughter are some of your best tools in your workbag for success! Laughter is everywhere. No matter which geographic area, country or culture you work in, you are guaranteed to encounter it. Laughter through humour (when used effectively), can prevent burnout and create a resilience to stress, release tension and relax people.[1] Relaxed and happy people are more creative,[2] open to working with each other and this boosts productivity. When you genuinely laugh with co-workers, clients or customers, there is connection and more reception to ideas. Positive sounds of laughter can trigger a response in the listener's brain and by priming them to smile or laugh, and aiding connection with the other person.[3] Shared laughter promotes relationship well-being.[4] Relaxation that results from a bout of laughter reduces the stress response, triggers the release of endorphins that help workers to feel more relaxed both physically and emotionally. Those who are high in humour character traits are reported to leverage higher levels of positive affect in stressful situations and see a potentially stressful event as a positive challenge rather than a threat. [5]

A genuine smile

Smiling with your eyes as well as your mouth (a Duchenne smile) can help lift your mood, calm you down, and help strengthen your connections with other people. Such a smile is quite persuasive and often associated with positive customer service experiences.[6]

Do you flash a fake smile at work? Perhaps to get through the working day or hide your inner unhappiness? Perhaps you have been asked to smile more at your customers? Research suggests that it may have unexpected consequences, such as worsening your mood and causing you to withdraw from the tasks at hand. Workers found to engage in fake smiling (known as 'surface acting') had worse moods as opposed to 'deep acting' where they generated genuine smiles through positive thoughts. Smiling for the sake of smiling can lead to emotional exhaustion and withdrawal and is not great for organisations. When workers smiled through deeper efforts (by cultivating pleasant thoughts and memories) their moods improved and their productivity increased. Hence a genuine smile can not only improve your mood but can make you more productive too. [7]

Exercise: Genuine smile practice

A genuine smile is a specific type of positive facial, allowing people to feel more at ease. Practise in a mirror or with a partner. First, visualise someone you deeply care for/love or picture, or recall an event or memory that brought you deep satisfaction and joy. This will aid natural happiness and positive feelings in you. You will know when your smile is genuine because you will feel happy and relaxed.

Laughter and teams

"Laughter occurs when people are comfortable with one another, when they feel open and free. And the more laughter there is, the more bonding occurs within the group." [8]

Laughter and humour can serve as a useful measure of just how healthy and well-functioning a team or workplace is. Laughter around the office likely indicates that people are getting along, are highly motivated and work in a positive, open and supportive atmosphere. Laughter can be viewed as the sound of bonding and collaboration, great signs of a productive team. A habit of genuinely smiling more at work can force your brain to associate this positivity with your workplace, therefore increasing the satisfaction that you feel with your job. Smiles are contagious and create harmony among co-workers. A warm smile to one co-worker can create a chain effect of kindness and warmth and convey confidence in your abilities.

Groups, laughter and success

"Groups work best when they have somebody who takes on the role of class clown. These are people that have the ability to pull everyone together, bridge gaps when tensions appear and really boost morale. We can all think of the person at work who fulfils this role, who makes us laugh and makes the job more enjoyable. People like being around them." [9] The study of isolated groups of people in extreme environments has shown that missions have led to success because of the presence of happy, humorous traits. One example is the Norwegian explorer Roald Amundsen who succeeded in reaching the South Pole, because the Norwegians had a jolly 'clown' figure on their team, who brought people together. Amundsen had a cook named Adolf Lindstrom, described as someone who laughed and kept up morale.

Happy people work harder

A team of economic researchers found that smiling contributed to a healthier work ethic in an office environment and that human happiness has large and positive effects on productivity. The team found "Happier workers ... were 12% more productive.

Unhappier workers were 10% less productive." Significantly, subjects who did not report higher levels of happiness were unable to demonstrate higher levels of productivity. The researchers reported that "human happiness has large and positive causal effects on productivity," and "positive emotions appear to invigorate human beings, while negative emotions have the opposite effect." [10]

Laughter, humour and leadership

One way to describe a great leader is one who seeks every opportunity to communicate and mentor others and clarify team objectives. [11]

The ability to use humor effectively has been identified both in the popular and the academic literature as an important aspect of "good" leadership .

As a leader, if you can access genuine smiles, you can contribute to healthy communication and draw people to you and generate positivity. A smile with an upbeat outlook can help others feel more relaxed and able to be themselves, fostering a nurturing work environment that supports others in excellence.

Studies have also found that dominant individuals such as the manager (or the tribal chief or the head of the family), use humour more than their subordinates. [12] This supports the scenario when everyone in the office laughs when the boss laughs. Controlling the laughter of a group can become a way of exercising power by controlling the emotional climate of the group. Laughter, like much human behaviour, is said to have evolved to change the behaviour of others. For example, in an embarrassing or threatening situation, laughter may serve as a calming gesture or as a way to deflect anger. If the threatening person joins the laughter, the risk of dispute may lessen.

The effective use of workplace humour to generate new ideas and stimulate intellectual progress is strongly associated with what has been labelled 'transformational' leadership. [13] Transformational leadership describes leaders who are said to model integrity and fairness, set clear goals, encourage, provide support and recognition, inspire people to buy into and deliver the vision set. Transformational leaders who utilise humour are more effective in winning trust and affecting commitment from their followers. With leaders who set clear expectations related to goals and rewards, humour increases their effectiveness. [14]

But not every leadership style is suited to employ humour, especially when aggressive humour is employed. In organisations, excessively aggressive humour could involve ridiculing others, and mild aggressive humour in the workplace includes sarcasm and teasing to humorously convey disapproving information to their followers (e.g. 'X, you seem so busy' to sarcastically convey a message that X is not putting in enough effort). Aggressive humour is a form of unfavourable and even hostile behaviour. For example, sarcasm is often associated with increased interpersonal conflict in a work group because it conveys disapproval, contempt and scorn humorously. A leader who has a strong sense of humour and tends to use aggressive humour leads to more behaviour that is deviant and creates the feeling of exclusion. For the targets of aggressive humour, the results are often negative impacts on private and professional life, such as related to performance, attendance, safety and health. [15, 16, 17]

Humour for career growth

A sense of humour, when appropriately used, can enhance workplace status and perception of one's competence.

The successful use of humour signals confidence and competence, which in turn increases the joke teller's status. If you are seen as genuinely funny at work, you could be more successful by appearing confident, competent and this increases status. Humour even influences behaviour. Workers who effectively use humour, are more likely to be elected as a group leader for a subsequent task. Successful joke telling takes competence and emotional intelligence.

However, inappropriate jokes signal low competence and despite high confidence, the low competence harms status. Sometimes humour can fail because it's inappropriate, not very funny or because it's overdone. [18]

Avoid using humour which your audience could find insulting or offensive in some way or inappropriate for the situation. Humour perceived as 'clownish' can get you noticed for the wrong reasons. Humour which is overly self-deprecating can negatively influence people's opinion of you, even if they find the humour itself amusing.

A few ground rules to keep humour at work appropriate:

- Never make a joke about gender, race, ethnicity, disability, orientation or any personal attribute of anyone.
- Keep it clean, never say anything lewd or sexual.
- Make smart jokes that ridicule no one and are not at anyone's expense.
- Leave out any humour and jokes related to politics, injuries, crime and death.
- Avoid dark humour. Stay away from jokes about harm coming to things that people around you are likely to hold dear, like kids and animals, or jokes that feel mean-spirited.
- If in any doubt, do not use the humour.

Exercise: Self-reflection break

- What does the sound of laughter at work mean to me?
- Would more laughter in my workplace make my work more enjoyable?
- Do I see leaders and co-workers laugh and use appropriate humour at my workplace?

Self-efficacy and laughter

Self-efficacy is the belief in one's capabilities to organise and execute the courses of action required to manage prospective situations. [19]

Self-efficacy is your belief in your ability to succeed and manage a particular situation and it affects your performance in the workplace. It is an important topic, as self-efficacy can have an impact on everything from mental well-being and behaviour to motivation and more. Your belief in your own ability to succeed plays a role in how you think, how you act and how you feel about your place at work and beyond. Self-efficacy determines what goals you choose to pursue, how you go about accomplishing those goals and how you reflect upon your own performance. [20]

The good news is that self-efficacy is a skill that you can improve and even in a fun way... using laughter! In a study, employees were engaged in a guided programme of non-humour-dependent laughter. It was found that the workers demonstrated a significant increase in several different aspects of self-efficacy, including self-regulation, optimism, positive emotions and social identification, and they maintained these gains at follow-up. Laughter has been found to improve self-efficacy AND lower the level of stress hormones in workers from different cultures, for example Danish, American and Indian employees. "Purposeful laughter is a realistic, sustainable, and generalisable intervention that enhances employees' morale, resilience, and personal efficacy beliefs." [21]

Creativity is enhanced by laughter and humour

"A playful, light-hearted, and humorous environment is especially helpful when ideas are incubating and newly hatched, the phase when they are most vulnerable to being snuffed out or even expressed because of being judged or self-censored." [22]

Humour can help people be more creative in problem solving. Laughter helps colleagues relax around each other and this creates a playful environment that cultivates curiosity and enhances creativity. I have noticed laughter and humour gives people permission to express their own unique creative voice more easily.

Laughter and humour provide a chance to see things from a new perspective and this aids divergent thinking. Divergent thinking (also called Creative or Horizontal Thinking) is a method used to generate creative ideas by exploring many possible solutions and is a spontaneous, free-flowing, non-linear thinking process. [23] Jokes and other types of humour use language or items incorrectly or see from different angles, in order to raise laughter, essentially a divergent thinking exercise. When you're thinking divergently, you're looking at things from new perspectives and finding new uses for common ideas and objects. Divergent thinking can rewrite rules and question everything. Humour uses and encourages divergent thinking.

"Laughter can help people solve problems that demand creative solutions, by making it easier to think more broadly and associate ideas/ relationships more freely." [24]

DID YOU KNOW? Dopamine (one of the four major chemicals in the brain that influence our happiness) released by a smile is involved in learning, processing and decision-making, allowing for heightened creativity.

Laughter and learning

Laughter stimulates many regions of the brain and, together with humour, this releases tension and leads to more creativity, which benefits teaching and learning. The inclusion of humour assists the promotion of understanding, holds the attention of students, creates a positive attitude to the subject matter and reduces anxiety. Humour, provided it is not used to excess, can increase attention and interest and helps to illustrate and reinforce what is being taught. [25]

DID YOU KNOW? Humour activates the brain's dopamine reward system, stimulating goal-oriented motivation and long-term memory. Humour can improve retention in students of all ages. [26]

Workplace laughter yoga

Laughter yoga is a great workplace well-being initiative; Google and BBC have organised laughter sessions leaving participants feeling happier and more relaxed. Opportunities to laugh together at work, can promote positive interactions, especially before having difficult or conflict-prone conversations. Shared laughter could be incorporated into staff meetings to make people feel more on the same page and aid productivity.

Laughter yoga is based on laughing with (not at) people using group activities and does not use joke telling. Both of these principles are useful to refer to when remembering to practise 'safe humour' in the workplace – humour that builds rather than divides relationships.

Laughter yoga consists of group activities to lengthen laughter, with zero yoga bendy positions and zero jokes. The yoga element refers to the healthy breath work that takes place with lengthened laughter. Sessions can be run seated or with movement. Prolonged laughter leads to more oxygen uptake which improves efficiency, mental focus and concentration. Furthermore, laughter yoga connects you with colleagues in a non-competitive environment and improves relationships. Lengthened laughter, in laughter yoga, can improve your self-efficacy for increased performance and provide opportunities for team bonding and team building. Laughter yoga is a fun way to generate optimism and positivity to cope with challenging times. [27]

Exercise: Workplace laughter session

Incorporate humour at work by organising a laughter session. Bring in a professional laughter facilitator/yoga laughter teacher to create a happier, healthier, more creative and productive office. A professional can set the right mood and facilitate so the session is suitable for everyone. Just be mindful that laughter after lunch is not always comfortable so arrange prior to lunch and then eat together for more social connection and bonding.

NASA, humour and recruitment

NASA has undertaken research and reported that a sense of humour will be vital for any team to keep morale high on a two-year trip to Mars which could happen in the 2030s. In the scientific paper 'Teamwork and Collaboration in Long-Duration Space Missions: Going to Extremes', the researchers reported that "humour, which stems from personality and may be influenced by cultural factors, is often cited as a benefit by spaceflight". Astronauts aboard the International Space Station reported that appropriate humour is a key factor in crew compatibility, conflict resolution, and coping – "humour and joking around continue to be huge assets and quickly defuse any problems" (astronaut journal entry). [28]

At your workplace, whether in the office, home or out and about – *"A good time to laugh is any time you can."*

Dr Madan Kataria [29]

Thank you for reading this chapter.

Onwards to find out how happy ageing can be accessed in a number of ways, whatever you age or circumstances.

"Prolonged laughter leads to more oxygen uptake which improves efficiency, mental focus and concentration."

Sam Rehan

CHAPTER 9
HAPPY AGEING

"Life is better when you're laughing."

Anonymous

What of ageing?

Ageing, a time to slow down and limit activities or a time to remain active, whatever your abilities and explore extra enjoyment? What part of us ages? In my previous role as a carer for seniors, I saw build-up of years in bodies but witnessed the magic and merriment of youth in many. Clients sharing sudden smiles and lengthy laughter created intense experiences. Happy emotional peaks engaged us in the moment and created a temporary deep bond, despite the difference in biological years.

At some point in life, many of us become concerned about ageing and want to know what to expect, what to avoid and what to do, to adapt. The term 'successful ageing' was made popular in 1980s to differentiate between usual ageing which describes functioning well, but with a high risk for disease and disability. [1] However this doesn't address that a disease-free older age is not possible for most people. Additionally, many elderly people regard themselves as happy and well, even in the presence of disease or disability. [2]

An exact definition of successful ageing is still outstanding. Other terms in use are positive ageing, healthy ageing and optimal ageing.

Happy ageing

"In interviews, the first question I get in America is always: 'What do you do to stay young?' I do nothing. I don't think aging is a problem. What irritates me a little is growing fatter. It irritates me that if I eat what I want to eat, it shows. Yes, my face has wrinkles. But I don't find it monstrous. I'm so surprised that the emphasis on aging here is on physical decay, when aging brings such incredible freedom. Now what I want most is laughs. I don't want to hurt anybody by laughing – there is no meanness to it. I just want to laugh."

Isabella Rossellini

It has been stated that laughter and humour positively affect satisfaction with the ageing process. The ability to laugh gave participants a sense of control over their situation. It is known that people who have a sense of control over their daily life are more satisfied with their housing arrangements, lives and selves, all of which are important to the process of ageing well. [3]

"Always keep your sense of humor. That's what I attribute my long life to. I think I'll die laughing. That's part of my program," said Jeanne Calment, whose age was well-documented, with a lifespan of 122 years and 164 days. Her longevity attracted media attention and medical studies of her health and lifestyle. [4]

Analysis of older adults reaching plus 90 years showed that there were certain attributes that are very important, including resilience, positivity, strong social support, engagement and confidence. Most of the older adults studied were still active, working regularly in their homes and on their land. They had a sense of purpose in life even after they reached old age. Happiness and satisfaction with life went up, and levels of depression and stress went down. [5]

Enjoying your life, a contributor to healthy ageing

Both smiling and laughing have a beneficial effect on your health and are signs that we are enjoying life. Happy people have been found to be more robust and fit and genes are said to only contribute one-fourth to one-third of your longevity. [6]

Exercise supports a longer healthier life, by increasing energy levels and overall health and directly reduces stress in a number of ways. It was reported that incorporating laughter into a physical activity programme for older adults led to older adults gaining additional benefits. A significant number found laughter to be an enjoyable addition to a traditional exercise programme, helped make exercise more accessible and enhanced their motivation to participate in other exercise classes. [7]

Savour any good health, because if we look hard enough, I believe we can always find health. In a hospice, I have asked clients "What part of your body is strong and healthy". Without exception, each person had a response ("my sense of smell, my sharp tongue, my toes"). I propose we take steps to maintain strength and keep body and mind strong by accessing as much happiness as we can.

Satisfaction and happiness have been used as the basis for defining successful ageing. Ageing can be thought of as disengaging, meaning a person desires to remove themselves from an active life. Or ageing can be active, where a person carries over activities and attitudes from middle age into later life. [8]

In my experience, laughter and smiles are valuable tools to keep us mentally and physically active and keep us engaged with ourselves and others. In care homes, I have seen people appear to wake up in the throes of group laughter. Speech may not be present but eyes sparkle and laughter sounds emerge and they re-engage with those present. With those more distant, touching of hands and sharing of smiles has brought out smiles, speech and laughter when no engagement was present. [9]

I believe, having the resources to laugh, share laughter and the effects that these practices have on how we age can, in fact, lead to a form of successful ageing, whatever your health or age. When we are laughing or smiling, there are no winners or losers in longevity or health.

Socialise with a smile

If laughter is medicine, it is also an important source of social well-being. Social laughter triggers the release of feel-good chemicals called endorphins. Endorphins interact with other brain chemicals which relieves pain and triggers feelings of pleasure and well-being.[10]

Social support can play a significant role in overall health as people age. Spending time with others can boost quality of life, and both physical and mental health. More than 1,100 seniors without dementia at baseline were measured on their social activity levels and then tested periodically on their cognitive functioning over a 12-year period. It was found that cognitive abilities declined 70% more slowly in individuals who had frequent social connections compared to those who had little social contact with others.[11]

If you are supporting someone to access more social contact, then consider connecting them with new learning. Perhaps some could use extra help getting set up for video chats or finding new sources of online connection. This itself can be a fun bonding experience and in itself continued contact. Perhaps you can take a class together. Greater technology use was reported to be associated with better self-rated health, lower depression and the potential to grow successful relationships among older adults.[12]

Making friends and connecting meaningfully with people who share similar interests is an important part of ageing and any stage of life. Research suggests a good way to make new friends is to smile.[13] Others are much more open to positive emotions when forming new bonds than they are to negative ones. Caution – the smile must be sincere as most people can recognise a fake smile. Access a joyful memory, image or positive thoughts, to generate a genuine smile. A smile is a powerful way to create social rapport whatever your age. You can instantly create a connection that allows both of you to release feel-good chemicals in your brain and increase the chances of you both living longer, healthier lives.

Exercise: Retain and expand social connections

Find ways to engage with more people for social support. Perhaps enlist the help of family, carers, friends and organisations so they can aid your quest. Some ways more social contact can be sought include group exercise classes and community groups such as senior centres. Another example to get connected with more people is to find an organisation you are passionate about and volunteer. Social contact maximises friendship, health and happiness. As much as possible, find ways to smile with others to aid connection and sharing. Access positive memories and joyful thoughts to access authentic smiles.

Nature for health and happiness

"In every walk with nature one receives far more than he seeks."

John Muir

How much time do you spend looking at greenery? Perhaps in a garden or viewing a green scene from your window? A huge body of research has shown that being in nature, living near nature, or even viewing nature in paintings and videos can have positive impacts on us, helping us to access position emotions and triggering a calming response in our bodies. Looking at plants, trees and greenery reduces stress, boosts mood, improves concentration and more.[14]

DID YOU KNOW? Biophilia is our natural desire to be connected with nature. [15]

Research has shown that individuals who walked in natural surroundings had lower levels of frustration and arousal and were calmer than those who took the urban routes such as a shopping street. [16] A large study In Denmark included nearly a million people and found a positive connection between green space and mental health. [17]

It was reported that in order to reap the health benefits of nature, the optimal amount of time to spend in green spaces (i.e. urban parks, the woods or beaches) is two hours per week. The findings were consistent across different groups including older adults and those with long-term health issues. Interestingly, it did not matter how the two hours of nature contact a week was achieved (e.g. one long vs several shorter visits/week). [18]

Watching a short video is another way to harness happiness. You can access some of the mental health benefits of going outside and experiencing nature by viewing nature videos. This has been found to increase happiness, contentment and boost other positive emotions in a study that surveyed more than 7,500 participating viewers from the US, UK, Singapore, India, South Africa and Australia. [19]

What if you are not able to access a nature video and have zero greenery to view through your window? Even a short mini break of looking at a desk plant for three minutes was reported to decreases stress. [20]

Our access to nature doesn't even have to be real for us to access some of the benefits associated with green spaces. Looking at still images of nature is a 'natural' stimulus to lower our stress levels. [21]

Exercise: Green laughter

Use the colour green and nature as a trigger to remember to smile or access laughter. This could range from watering and viewing greenery at home, looking at photos of nature, watching a nature video or being outdoors.

Blue for well-being

"An ocean breeze puts a mind at ease."

Unknown

How does viewing a water feature such as a fountain make you feel? What about a walk beside a river or an ocean view? Blue spaces have been proven to make you feel happier. 'Blue' spaces are environments with running or still water and have found to be especially beneficial for healthy ageing. Proximity to water has been reported to be associated with more pronounced improvements in well-being. "Accessibility to everyday green and blue spaces encourages seniors to simply get out the door. This in turn motivates them to be active physically, spiritually and socially, which can offset chronic illness, disability and isolation." [22]

A large research study involved 20,000 smartphone users, who recorded their sense of well-being and their immediate environment at random intervals. Marine and coastal margins were found by some distance to be the happiest locations. [23]

Why our love for close proximity to water for happiness and relaxation? One theory is that water and access to coastlines played an important role in human evolution and the sounds, smells and sights of seas, lakes and rivers are naturally therapeutic. Pleasing environments make us feel better because what we see, hear and experience at any moment is changing not only your mood for the better, but impacts your body positively too.

Even visiting an aquarium has been found to promote a better mood and participants scored as high on measures of well-being as those who spent time outside in a natural environment. [24]

Exercise: Blue laughter

Access running or still water outside. For example, swimming, visiting a waterfront area or a water fountain. Sit or walk beside the water and use water in nature as a trigger to remember to access positive emotions: smiling and accessing laughter.

Imagery

Creating pictures in the mind (imagery) is a simple, and powerful tool for creating positive change. Perhaps you want to spend more time in nature or visit the sea with friends. You can imagine these scenarios happening (or anything else that you would like in your life) with positive emotions. Following this up and writing about yourself and the imagined happiness and practising this action is effective as an intentional exercise. Research showed that this exercise acts as a motivation and stimulant for people to achieve the life they want to live and obtain pleasure like they imagined they would. [25]

Exercise: Imagined-self technique

Seated, eyes closed and comfortable, imagine yourself in the future. Perhaps six months or a year from now and you have achieved everything you want for your life with all the people you want to share it with. Immerse yourself into that imagined self of yours. Ask yourself while imagining, 'What will it feel like when I achieve this in my life?' Aim to impersonate the happiness and positivity that you think you might feel then. Perhaps smiling and laughing with close ones. Next, ask yourself what you can do to get to that stage in life, and write down your responses. Reread your words and imagine regularly to access more positivity.

Gifting positivity with visualisation

"Making money is a happiness; making other people happy is a superhappiness."

Muhammad Yunus

For centuries, the greatest thinkers have suggested that happiness is found in helping others.

Endorphins, the feel-good brain chemical that gets produced during exercise, is what athletes refer to as a runner's high. The 'helpers high' has been confirmed in various studies and consists of positive emotions that arise when you help someone. [26] The act of giving or acts of kindness, produce a natural mild version of a morphine high. What is important is that it's not the size of the help we offer but the gesture of genuinely wanting to help.

DID YOU KNOW? Helping isn't just linked to a healthier life but to a longer one. A survey of more than 7,000 older adults found that frequent volunteering was linked to longevity.[27] Regardless of our situation, we can still give, even if it is with a smile when we are alone, as shown in the exercise below.

Exercise: Gifting smiles with visualisations

Giving to others generates positive emotions in us for better health. We can still give to others in a visualisation exercise, helping us to remain connected to others, whether they are close to us or not. Close your eyes and visualise yourself giving a generous smile (or even laughter) to someone very close to you, perhaps even a pet. Now open your eyes. How do you feel? Imagine that person smiling back and laughing with you. Next, close your eyes and visualise yourself giving a generous smile to someone who is an acquaintance or someone you recently met and feel that same response and laughter. You can expand this exercise by repeating this exercise and visualise yourself giving a generous smile to someone who you think is really in need of help and feel that response and laughter. Practise this regularly.

Gratitude and happiness

"If you want to find happiness, find gratitude."

Steve Maraboli

Gratitude practices have proven benefits in increasing happiness and satisfaction. [28]

Gratitude helps people feel more positive emotions, improve their health and build strong relationships. Research has shown regular practice of gratitude exercises enhance our attention to what is good in our lives and helps us derive more pleasure from social relationships. [29]

Exercise: Three good things

Write down three positive things that happened during your day, things you are thankful for and what made you happy. This can spark smiling, which is the beginning of laughter. The exercise can deepen if you can add who was involved and the feelings generated. For example, 'I am thankful that my friend Lisa took the time to connect with me by writing me a wonderful letter. Reading it made me feel lighter, made me smile and grateful that she took the time out to do that.' It helps cement the habit, if you can do this exercise, daily after an action you take every day, perhaps after dinner and before bedtime.

Mindfulness

My favourite definition of mindfulness is "maintaining a moment-by-moment awareness of our thoughts, feelings, bodily sensations, and surrounding environment, through a gentle, nurturing lens." [30]

Mindfulness has existed as a concept for over two thousand years. Findings have demonstrated that mindfulness practices are strongly linked with life satisfaction and overall well-being. [31, 32]

A mindfulness practice involves paying attention to your breathing and tuning into your body's physical sensations in a given moment, such as sights, sounds and smells that ordinarily pass you by. Becoming more aware of the present moment can help us enjoy the world around us more. Another important part of mindfulness is an awareness of our thoughts and feelings as they happen moment to moment. This helps us to stand back from our thoughts and start to see their patterns. We can start to notice when our thoughts are taking over and notice if they are helpful thoughts or not. With regular practice, we can understand ourselves better and reduce negative thought patterns.

Exercise: Inner smile mindfulness practice

We can extend a smile to ourselves and access positive emotions that we experience when we smile to another. Find a comfortable place to sit or lie down. Close your eyes and bring your attention to your breath. Imagine that on each breath out, you are releasing all tension from your body. Generate a smile by allowing a joyful or funny memory or picture to appear to you. Perhaps you can imagine someone you care for or love is smiling at you. Allow time for an image to come to the surface, for a real smile. As you continue to smile, breathe deeply and slowly. Continue to imagine that on each breath out, you are releasing any held tension from your body. Continue to smile. Bring your attention to the space between your eyebrows. Imagine your smile is adding warm happy energy to this area. Let your body relax. You will now picture the warm energy of your smile (inner smile) moving from the space between your eyebrows to cascade like a gentle waterfall through your entire body so it is soothed by this smiling, warm energy. Allow the warm inner smile to drift where it wants, or direct it to any place you would like more relaxation and ease. Imagine this warm, smiling energy spreading slowly to each part of your body and as it does, you can picture organs, tissues and bones smiling. Allow the smile to settle where you want in your body, to relax and nourish you. Breathe gently into any part of your body, where your inner smile may need a bit more support. Allow your inner smile to flow as you wish. When you're ready to bring the meditation to a close, keep your smile and very gently open your eyes. Take several deep breaths and relax. Gently bring your awareness back to your breath, body, and continue to smile. Breathe gently and bring your attention back to the room. Stay seated or lying down for a few minutes or more.

Humour and increased appetite

"Laughter is brightest where food is best."

Irish proverb

Depression (major depressive disorder) is a common medical illness that negatively affects how you feel, the way you think and how you act. Depression causes feelings of sadness and/or a loss of interest in activities once enjoyed. It is also treatable.[33] Appetite changes have long been recognised as common diagnostic features of depression. [34]

Poor appetite is a common problem in older people and there are many reasons why people lose their appetite. They may be in chronic pain or develop wasting diseases. This can lead to depression and, combined with a lack of physical activity, loss of appetite, and negatively impacts well-being. Proper nutrition and adequate calories are crucial for people to maintain physical and mental well-being.[35]

It was reported that humour can create some of the same changes in the body's chemistry as a short session physical exercise. The same hormonal changes that follow exercise are thought to boost appetite. The research did not prove that laughing improves appetite or fitness but could improve treatments for people who can lose their appetites. "It may provide... further potential options for patients who cannot use physical activity to normalise or enhance their appetite." [36]

I often choose to laugh with clients prior to lunch, as laughing on a full stomach isn't always pleasant. Verbally, it is reported quite frequently (in a range of adult ages) that they are hungry post-laughter (hence I carry healthy snacks, such as dates, to alleviate this). It would be useful for researchers to look at appetite levels post-laughter sessions to determine any positive changes.

Restorative sleep

How much sleep do you get most nights? It is recommended that for healthy individuals (and those not suffering from a sleep disorder): adults (26–64) obtain 7–9 hours while older adults (65+) should sleep between is 7–8 hours. Like good diet and exercise, sleep is a critical component to overall health. [37]

Significant changes in sleep accompany ageing for most adults and there are a variety of potential causes. Ageing is accompanied by a variety of sleep complaints and sleep disorders. Sleep can become more fragmented, lighter with an increase in the number of awakenings.[38] Poor sleep is related to memory decline and research has repeatedly shown that in older individuals, poor sleep and short sleep time is one of the strongest predictors of falls. Individuals who sleep more poorly or sleep less have a lower survival rate, a higher mortality rate, than individuals who sleep more and suggests sleep has some rejuvenation or restorative function, which is important in terms of longevity in human beings.[39]

It was reported that laughing in the evening helped the body to produce more melatonin (the hormone released by the brain at sleep onset).[40] Another study showed positive effects of laughter therapy (delivered with movement and physical activities) on sleep and depression for patients in hospital. [41]

In another study, older adults were enrolled in laughter therapy. Mental health, depression, self-reported physical health, and sleep quality were measured before and after the laughter therapy intervention. The researchers reported: *"Laughter therapy is considered to be [a] useful, cost-effective, and easily-accessible intervention that has positive effects on depression, insomnia, and sleep quality in the elderly."* [42]

Many of my clients have reported that light-hearted reading or watching comedy has helped them move towards more relaxation at bedtime, and supports them unwinding at the end of a day. Laughter can help gently nudge you towards lightness and aid sleep. More often than not, clients have fed back that a laughter yoga session has aided their sleep that night and reported sleeping more deeply and longer.

Laughter supports the skin

"Laughter is the sun that drives winter from the human face."

Victor Hugo

When you laugh regularly, deeply and for longer, your skin benefits. There is a temporary increase in blood flow which causes the capillaries close to the skin to dilate in a similar way to when we exercise. [43] Laughing increases the blood supply to your cheeks, nourishes your skin and makes your face radiate. Laughter dilates the inner lining of our blood vessels and helps improves circulation. When we laugh heartedly, we take in more oxygen and this is beneficial to your skin.[44] We are all familiar with how readily children burst into unrestrained laughter... laughing is related to youth and beauty. You're actually perceived as better looking when you smile! Researchers asked subjects to rate smiling and attractiveness. They found that both men and women were more attracted to images of people who made eye contact and smiled than those who did not.[45]

Water

How much of us is water? Water comprises from 75% body weight in infants to 55% in the elderly. [46] Even mild dehydration negatively affects mental performance (for example memory, attention and concentration) and increases feelings of tiredness.[47]

Ageing typically leads to a 5–10% increase in total body fat, and a decrease in total body water of an equal magnitude. Normal ageing changes increase the risk for fluid imbalance and dehydration. Elderly residents are less capable of maintaining fluid balance compared with younger people.[48] In an elderly 70-kg male, this can account for a reduction of total body water of as much as 7–8 litres compared with a young male of the same weight.[49] In the UK, the government guidelines recommend six to eight cups or glasses a day.[50]

Your water drinking habit can be supplemented by engaging with a positive based activity such as mindfulness and a smile, to access better health. Mindfulness is simply noticing what is happening right now and paying attention in a particular way.

Exercise: Drinking water with mindfulness and a smile

How you drink water can affect how your body and mind responds. Here is a recommended daily exercise to use with one of your recommended glasses of water. Water drinking twinned with positivity and smiling.

First sit down. Being seated helps you access more relaxation and helps your digestion. Take a moment to observe the water in the glass. Are there bubbles? Is there light and colour reflecting in the water? Sip your water slowly. How does your water taste? Consider the texture. How do you feel if you let the water linger for a few moments in your mouth? Continue to sip the water slowly at your own pace. Once you finish your glass, take a moment to be thankful. Raise a smile with gratitude that you have access to clean plentiful water. Let your smile linger as you extend the gratitude by giving thanks for the pipes and plumbing that carries the water to your home or the people and equipment involved in bottling your water. Extend the gratitude to your body, as it will use this glass of water to support your functioning and health. How do you feel after drinking your glass of water?

Grief and humour

"Humour was a big part of my live, and it is still part here with me, while I am dying. Laughter helps me to cope and I welcome it."

Keith W.

Grief is often first associated with death. However, grief and mourning can come with the loss of a job, ending of a relationship, a rift with someone close and grown-up children leaving home and more. More often than not, people use humour in times of grief. Laughter helps us to put the circumstances into perspective and help us to feel safer. Humour can be used to make a difficult situation a bit easier to manage, for us and those around us.[51]

When we are in the depths of grief, it is hard to imagine that we will ever smile again, let alone laugh, but even during times of great difficulty positive emotions can be accessed and are highly regarded. Recently bereaved spouses reported a great deal of importance on having humour and happiness in their daily lives. Positive emotions (including laughter) were experienced relatively early in the course of their bereavement journey. Even though their spouse had died approximately only four months previously the widowed participants valued and experienced these positive feelings.[52]

"Grief leaves no joy and everything seems pointless. Laughter did come; unexpectedly. A bouncing dog made me light up. Alongside the memories of my gone-too-soon beautiful daughter, I laughed and smiled,

remembering that she would have delighted in this huge jumpy dog and I laughed for her and for me."

Name withheld

Laughter is a useful tool for those involved in hospice work, care-giving and those who work with the dying. Humorous interactions have found to be a prevalent part of everyday hospice work. Humour was found to be present in 85% of 132 observed nurse-based hospice visits. And that 70% of the humour was initiated by the patient and included spontaneous humour and humour that was frequent.[53]

Laughter and humour help to ease stress for care givers and in a group provides opportunities for colleagues to bond and is a factor in longevity in hospice work.[54]

Resilience is said to be a quality necessary to succeed in nursing, because the conditions can be so adverse. One of the strategies to develop resilience in nurses is described as maintaining positivity through laughter, optimism and positive emotion.[55]

It is important to remember that grief is unique and humour at such a time seems to surprise people, but this type of reaction is normal. You may see someone rely on laughter at times, but this doesn't mean that they don't also spend a good amount of time with other emotions. All emotions are valid and support healing.

Exercise: Accessing humour in difficult times

If you spend most of your day in bed or house-bound, here are some examples of things to help you access more humour:

- Ask funny or positive friends to visit.
- Contact people and let them know you want to access more humour and enlist them to help you.
- Locate or ask someone who knows you to recommend

comedy films, audio recordings and reading you would enjoy.

- Put up visuals of funny and positive-emotion-provoking images.
- Frame photos of you and your family or friends having fun.
- Surround yourself with things that please, nurture and remind you that there is still joy in living, even if the challenges are great. Perhaps create a 'smile album' containing photos of loved ones smiling and laughing.

Breath

"Breathing creates the platform on which everything else – health, happiness, cognitive ability and elevated performance, success and influence – is built."

Alan Watkins

We usually breathe an average of 13 pints/7 litres of air every minute, but how much do you think about your breath? Many of us do not give a second thought about the way we breathe. Our breathing affects our physical and mental health and our emotional balance and well-being. Although you can control your breathing, most of the time it is automatic. 90% of our energy comes from oxygen and around 70% of our toxins are released from our body through our breath.[56]

Deep breathing activates our relaxation response (the opposite of the fight or flight response) and aids to release muscle tension and reduce stress. The quality of our breath affects our mental state. Increased intake of oxygen, helps us move away from negative thought patterns, concentrate and memorise. Deeper breathing results in an increased blood flow in the digestive tract and together with a calmer body system, improves overall digestion.[57]

Breath improves the cardiovascular system (the system that moves blood, oxygen and nutrients through the body comprising the heart, blood and blood vessels). In one study of heart attack patients, 100% of the patients were chest breathers whose breathing involved no diaphragm or belly expansion.[58]

Exercise: Extend the breath out and smile

This is my go-to breathing technique when I want to feel more calm, quickly.

It is the out-breaths that stimulate the relaxation response. A breathing technique with longer out-breaths than in-breaths, send signals to the brain to calm down. The following is a breathing technique that has been around a long time and I have added a smile to support the relaxation that takes place. Breathe in for a count of seven and then breathe out for a count of 11. Use belly breathing:

Place one hand on your upper chest and the other on your belly, just below your rib cage. Breathe in slowly through your nose, letting the air in deeply, towards your lower belly. The hand on your chest should remain still, while the one on your belly should rise. Your belly moves out (sideways too) as you breathe in. Gently pull in your tummy as you breathe out slowly through pursed lips (similar to blowing on hot food) with a soft smile. The hand on your belly should move down to its original position.

If easier initially, you can adjust your breathing so you breathe in for three and breathe out for five, or breathe in for five and breathe out for seven. The key is that the out-breath is longer than the in-breath. Close your eyes if you wish and add an ever-so-gentle smile to your pursued lips. Bring your attention to a joyful memory or positive thought to access a genuine smile. Continue for a few minutes or longer. Aim to practice for a few times each day for relaxation.

Gratefully laugh today, each and every day.

Treasure the laughter in you and your companions, for to be connected to people who make eye contact with you and laugh with you, is priceless.

PART TWO

SUPPORT

"It takes community to maintain a human."

Earon Davis

"Today, is the loudest I have laughed for 36 years. I am 50 but I haven't laughed this loud in 36 years. You know how I remember that? When I was 14 years old, a group of older girls laughed at me and said that I had an awful laugh. From that day onwards, I quietened my laugh and laughed behind my hand. Today, with you all, I could embrace my laugh fully."

Mick

Laughter is not always straight forward and, for many, it can be tinged with difficulty. People have approached me in confidence and shared their social anxiety around group laughter, memories of laughter and being bullied. A client shared that the thought of being laughed at by a stranger was so strong it prevented them from leaving the house. Some medical conditions can cause laughter to be unpredictable and uncontrollable. In this section, I share information and helpful support that can be accessed outside of this book.

Note that the information in this section is not intended for professional diagnosis.

What does the sound of laughter mean to you?

How do you feel when you hear laughter from an individual? From a group of people? Can you laugh or does the sound and subject bring up hesitation or more? Generally, laughter is perceived as a positive behaviour. However, memories of laughter can be tinged with unpleasant memories or even fear. How many of us have experienced being laughed at and still recoil at the unpleasant thoughts? Learning about laughter may have brought up anxiety. Sometimes when laughter is directed at others it can be used for aggression and to hurt another person. When people laugh for the purposes of mocking, humiliating or bullying another, this is malicious behaviour that can affect someone long past the incident. The sound of laughter can bring up unpleasant memories in you or another individual. Is it currently difficult for you to laugh, hear laughter or participate in laughter with others?

Laughter and social anxiety

Social anxiety disorder, also called social phobia, is an overwhelming fear of social situations and can have a big impact on your life. Public situations of any kind may induce this disorder which is often expressed as a fear of being the centre of attention, or of others noticing the sufferer's anxious behaviour. The physical manifestations of this phobia include blushing, shaking and sweating, etc. It is one of the most common of the anxiety disorders, affecting around one in ten people in the UK and there are a range of treatments that can help. [1]

The Social Anxiety Institute recognises the benefits of laughter to overcome social anxiety. "The inclusion of laughter in the therapy group is very helpful, and the knowledge that there are laughter clubs throughout the world can serve as adjunct therapy for social anxiety." Dr Thomas A. Richards currently runs treatment programmes at the Social Anxiety Institute and is a leading clinical authority on the treatment of social anxiety disorder. Dr Richards uses laughter in the CBT therapy groups for social anxiety disorder. [2]

Access group laughter from home

If attending a group laughter session is difficult for you right now, there are some other options to participate in laughter with others. For a number of years, online video laughter clubs have operated. You can mute your video (no need to show your face if you choose) and without a need to travel or provide your name, you can login and hear weekly laughter sessions with live callers. In a similar manner, telephone laughter hotlines exist. There is no requirement to provide your name or details. Do check details and the cost of the call before participating. Laughter clubs can be found with an internet search or enlist a friend to help you find a suitable online group laughter club. Alternatively, some therapists provide one-to-one laughter sessions to aid social anxiety and help individuals overcome their fear. These can take place online or face to face. Do check the therapist is insured and registered. Many therapists will offer a free short consultation so you can gauge if it's someone you would like to work with.

Laughing and coughing

When you have a good laugh, small droplets of saliva can enter your upper respiratory system. The body does not like this happening as any 'foreign substance' in your airways brings with it the risk of a chest infection, so the cough reflex is triggered in order to remove it from your respiratory system. It is normal to have some coughing after a hard laugh. The nerves that are involved in the laughing reflex are the same nerves that are involved in the coughing reflex. Therefore, triggering of one of these reflexes (laughing) can cause spill over into the other reflex (coughing).[3] I have noted this occurring with individuals, at most my laughter sessions. If you have fits of coughing also at other times (not just while laughing) then this is something you might want to have investigated.

If you experience any discomfort or pain during laughter, seek medical advice.

Laughter and tears

In many instances, tears are produced when someone laughs too hard because the body is trying to balance itself in response to strong emotions. It has also been suggested that people cry while laughing because of too much pressure around the tear ducts due to the body shaking during strong laughter. Some evidence indicates the same part of the brain controls both crying and laughing. [4]

Perhaps you have experienced it or witnessed a friend or family member start weeping after laughter. Why do humans cry in this way? Laughter can help bring about emotional release. When we feel joy, grief and sadness can come up to be expressed. A good cry is normal and is often healing as it reduces stress and helps us return to a calm state. Like laughter, crying is beneficial, has a soothing effect and can help you balance your own emotions, calm yourself and reduce your own distress. [5], [6]

"I didn't expect to cry. I wasn't feeling sad but realised I had old stuff that needed to come up. The laughter helped me to shed tears that needed to be cried. I felt better."

Mother of two

Gelotophobia

"I would love to come to your laughter class, I have heard great things, but I can't. I know it's group laughter and people laugh together, but I will feel they will be laughing at me."

Name withheld

Some people greatly fear laughter and without obvious reasons. They relate laughter they hear, to be directed at themselves. The fear of being laughed at or made to appear ridiculous is termed 'gelotophobia' and is a type of social phobia. Gelotophobia (from the Greek gelos meaning laughter) means that the mere sight of a smile or hearing laughter from afar is enough to raise anxiety. Fear and shame are the dominant negative emotions reported by individuals who are highly gelotophobic and they may suffer from low self-esteem and may avoid social situations. [7] Gelotophobes are susceptible to 'false alarms', i.e. misinterpreting friendly and innocent laughter as malicious and threatening. For example, a researcher describes an individual who couldn't even sit in front of another person in public and would always wait for the next bus if no seat in the last row was free, in case someone would sit behind him and laugh. [8]

Academic research into people with gelotophobia started in 2008. The phobia is thought to be caused by negative emotional experiences. It can also co-present with mental health and neurological conditions, like social anxiety and Asperger's syndrome. [9] Gelotophobia has been found to exist in many cultures and may affect as much as 13% of the global population. [10] The symptoms of gelotophobia are very similar to other specific phobias and will often include: constantly listening out for people's comments, panic attacks, inability to relax, problems concentrating and being quick tempered, and sweating excessively. Gelotophobia benefits from the same sort of therapies used to address other phobias, such as cognitive' (thinking)-based talking therapies as well as therapies based on 'emotional' content such as EMDR.[11]

PBA – unpredictable and uncontrollable emotional displays of laughing

Pseudobulbar affect (PBA) is a condition that's characterised by episodes of sudden uncontrollable and inappropriate laughing or crying. An individual with PBA experiences emotional eruptions that are disconnected from their inner feelings of happiness or sadness. Although sometimes the emotional displays may be prompted by something funny or sad, the fits of laughter or tears may be particularly intense and last an inappropriately long time.

Pseudobulbar affect typically occurs in people with certain neurological (brain, spine or nerves) conditions or injuries, which might affect the way the brain controls emotion. PBA is not a common condition but is thought to affect as many as 7 million people who have neurodegenerative diseases and neurological conditions such as the following: Parkinson's disease, Multiple sclerosis (MS), Lou Gehrig's disease (ALS), stroke, traumatic brain injury (TBI) and Alzheimer's disease/ other types of dementia.

Symptoms can range from mild and occasional to debilitating and constant. Outbursts can occur several times a day and last between a few seconds to a few minutes. Individuals report sudden and unpredictable onsets, which some describe as a seizure.

People who experience PBA often experience frustration, embarrassment, worry and confusion about their inappropriate displays of emotion. The condition may interfere with relationships, social activities and employment. Individuals living with PBA are generally aware of the inappropriateness of the response but have no voluntary control over the behaviour. Onlookers may sometimes confuse PBA sufferers' emotional outbursts with mental illness, particularly because patients cannot explain their behaviour. The condition is not widely recognised and thus is underdiagnosed. There is medical treatment available for PBA. [12, 13, 14]
If you think you have PBA, talk to your doctor.

Support groups and where to get help

Talking therapies

If you are struggling with past memories or a current situation, talking therapies can help. Talking therapies are referred to as counselling, talking treatments or psychological therapies. Cognitive behavioural therapy (CBT) is a talking therapy that can help you manage your problems by changing the way you think and behave. You can refer yourself directly for talking therapies or ask for a referral via your medical practitioner.

The British Association for Counselling and Psychotherapy (BACP) provide guidance on how to find a therapist and provide a register of therapists who are qualified and works to professional standards.
BACP: www.bacp.co.uk/

If you are struggling with anxiety and depression

Speak to your doctor or medical practitioner

The NHS: www.nhs.uk/conditions/social-anxiety/

Some organisations that can provide support in the UK:

Anxiety UK: www.anxietyuk.org.uk/

Mind: /www.mind.org.uk/

YoungMinds: www.youngminds.org.uk/

The Social Anxiety Institute (socialanxietyinstitute.org) contains over one hundred articles on social anxiety. Dr Thomas A. Richards lived with this disorder himself until, using cognitive behavioural therapy, he overcame it and went on to become a psychologist. He also heads the non-profit Social Anxiety Association.

Pseudobulbar affect (PBA)

More information: https://www.mstrust.org.uk/a-z/pseudobulbar-affect-pathological-laughing-and-crying

https://www.pbainfo.org/about-pba

FINAL WORDS

"I just try to live every day as if I've deliberately come back to this one day to enjoy it as if it was the full final day of my extraordinary, ordinary life."

Tim Lake, About Time

In the movie *About Time*, Bill Nighy's character has a way of living out each day; the first time to experience each day's inherent unpredictability and stress, and the second time to appreciate its small joys and special moments. My aim is to live each day once, in the fullness of authentic joy, smiles and laugh whenever possible and share. That is, genuine laughter and smiles intersecting with other emotions, which are all valid because we feel them.

When we laugh together in happiness, we are equal in that moment, there is no authority and we reveal our best. Shared laughter is a revitalising reward and a powerful light in our humanity. There is much still to be uncovered around the act of laughing and greater understanding may reveal knowledge, to further aid and support us, through the journey of our life.

QUOTES BY SAM REHAN

*Laugh for pleasure and peace,
and access calm and clarity within.*

*Power up your positivity and do the best you can,
with what you have today.*

*Keep going... It's a balance between focused
work and deliberate rest.*

*We are all in a storm but in different boats and the
best thing we can do? Be kind to each other.*

*If we can strive and continue to succeed, we can serve and
support ourselves, and our community.*

Laughter is a healthful link between surviving and thriving.

*If you cannot laugh in this moment, smile. If you can't smile
in this moment, then move your body in any way you can.
Notice your thoughts lessen and yourself soften.*

*Can I be angry and laugh at the same time? No.
Laughter is a powerful tool for love, peace and relaxation.*

*Smile with your heart, smile with your eyes
and fall into life's joyful surprise.*

“

Celebrate the good that surrounds you, say a thank you and serve yourself a smile.

Frequently flex your laughter muscle. You don't exercise once and consider yourself fit. Laughter is a practice.

Laughter is play, with movement, pleasure and peace to strength the mind, body, and enjoy release.

Nestle in nature for calm and clarity. Green spaces replenish our mental and physical energy.

There is never enough time to do everything, but there is always enough time to do the most important things and one of those things is laughing with your fellow man.

Play is part of our being and what better way to play but laugh regularly?

The beauty is that if we can't laugh, we smile and if we can't smile, we can soften, even so slightly.

In times of stress, smiling and laughter can provide breathing space for more security and strength to spring forth.

GET IN TOUCH

Thank you for reading this book. It would mean a lot to Sam if you could leave an honest review on Amazon or Goodreads.

Sam would love to hear how laughter supports you and your laughter journey.

Access more wellbeing techniques and tips at www.samrehan.com

Get in touch if you would like to work with Sam. She provides motivational energising talks and health boosting fun workshops for people of all backgrounds, abilities and work sectors. She shares positivity and practical methods from her 30 years work and life experiences. Sam uplifts and energise everyone, with accessible well-being techniques and straightforward science. Happier healthier people achieve more at work and beyond.

'If I can meet you where you are right now and evoke enthusiasm, then I can help you experience education that is possible for you'

- Sam Rehan

Sam lives in the UK but is globally active.
Contact Sam Rehan:

laughmore@samrehan.com
www.samrehan.com

ACKNOWLEDGMENTS

Thank you to all my loved ones – family and friends who, in so many countless ways, have aided my personal journey and growth and ultimately led to this book. We meet people for a reason, season or a lifetime...

Sharon Cresswell, every phone call and get-together makes me happy, nourishes me and inspires me to keep climbing to better things. Thank you for the strong accountability and your gentle kind strong support throughout the journey of this book. Your friendship and acceptance of where I am, strengthens me to no end. 'I never knew what a friend was until I met Geordi. He spoke to me as though I were human. He treated me no differently from anyone else. He accepted me for what I am. And that, I have learned, is friendship.'

Star Trek The Next Generation.

Adeline Garman, you are a true friend indeed. Thank you for believing in me and continually bringing out the best in me. Thank you for being there and checking in on me regularly even when you are swamped. "Friendship isn't about who you've known the longest, it's about who walked in to your life, said 'I'm here for you' and PROVED it".

Unknown

Pauline Westrop, there are friends, there is family, and then there are friends that become family. Thank you for being my rainbow. 'Try to be a rainbow in someone's cloud'

Maya Angelou

Anna Maria Donfrancesco...The eternal wise woman with a heart full of grace. Thank you for lighting my way and inspiring me greatly. 'To shine your brightest light is to be who you truly are'.

Roy T. Bennett

Laura Bettini, forever friends. Thank you for your strength and love. I AM GRATEFUL "In the sweetness of friendship let there be laughter, for in the dew of little things the heart finds its morning and is refreshed."

Khalil Gibran

Victoria Cresswell...Thank you for bringing new energy to my soul every time we speak. Thank you for your infinite wisdom and huge heart. 'How far that little candle throws his beams! So shines a good deed in a weary world.'

William Shakespeare, The Merchant of Venice

Karen Abi-Karam, Tracey Campbell and Sally Waite... each new friendship can make you a new person, because it opens up new doors inside of you. Thank you for opening new doors inside me and the joyful encounters. I look forward to more. 'Appreciation is a wonderful thing. It makes what is excellent in others belong to us as well.'

Voltaire

Geraldine Lowe, Thank you for your friendship, your big heart and selfless support. 'There's nothing like a really loyal, dependable, good friend. Nothing.'

Jennifer Aniston

Lorna Urwin-Wright for your wisdom, treasured talks and heartfelt sharing. 'In the right light, at the right time, everything is extraordinary'.

Aaron Rose

Carol Hilaire, I treasure all the help and support you have shown me over the years. A friend indeed and eternally grateful for your kindness and love. 'I appreciate you more because of the road I've traveled. My story brought me to you and I wouldn't revise a word of my past if it led me anywhere but to your door.'

Aaron Polson

Wendy Cooper, you provided light in time of need. So thankful for your kindness and care. When we share, our shared joy is double joy. 'The world is so empty if one thinks only of mountains, rivers & cities; but to know someone who thinks & feels with us, & who, though distant, is close to us in spirit, this makes the earth for us an inhabited garden.'

Goethe

Karin Bain and Marcus Bain, thank you beautiful souls. 'When we honestly ask ourselves which person in our lives means the most to us, we often find that it is those who, instead of giving advice, solutions, or cures, have chosen rather to share our pain and touch our wounds with a warm and tender hand."

Henri Nouwen

Maxine Temple, I appreciate your timeless wisdom. Thank you for all the help and support you provided me and the children and the gift of friendship when it was needed. 'When the world is so complicated, the simple gift of friendship is within all of our hands.'

Maria Shriver

Eirini, thank you for being there for me and the children when we needed support. I am grateful for your wisdom and generosity. 'Women's friendships are like a renewable source of power'.

Jane Fonda

To my mother, who shares her joy and smiles widely. Forever young, she lights up my life. As a child, I asked her what should I do when I grow up? She replied, "You can do anything you want." With her wisdom and support, I continue to soar with gratitude, success and light. My mum, you are one incredibly strong woman. I am in awe of you everyday. 'She is a friend of my mind. She gather me, man. The pieces I am, she gather them and give them back to me in all the right order."

Toni Morrison

Asma, you give cheerfully and accept gratefully. Always full of surprises and a staunch ally and a big light for me. With a zest for life, energy and presence, your ongoing support (since childhood) is more than you can realise. Thank you. 'You are part of my story, memory and scenery, thank you'.

kim Taehyung

Muzammil, thank you for your love and laughter. Sometimes the only thing you could do for people is to be there and you are there. Your huge caring nature is a blessing to me and to many others. 'Read a few books, you live a little, but help a few people, you live a lifetime'.

Abhijit Naskar

Sarwat, you go out and make some good things happen. Your nurturing and ability to step up and support others in need, is a huge inspiration to me. Keep going and I appreciate ALL that you do. 'Let us be grateful to the people who make us happy; they are the charming gardeners who make our souls blossom'.

Marcel Proust

Tayeba, thank you for steering me in a good direction and your wisdom, zest for life and unwavering support for my journey. Blessed, grateful and thankful for your support (practical and emotional). 'When we give cheerfully and accept gratefully, everyone is blessed'.

Maya Angelou

Mudassir, I appreciate and I am grateful for your helping hand. Thank you reminding me that it's not what we have in life, but who we have in our life that matters. 'Kind words can be short and easy to speak, but their echoes are truly endless.

Mother Teresa

And last but not least, James Willis at spiffingcovers.com. Thank you for seeing my full vision for this book and aiding my publishing journey. 2020 underwent a big change but you soldiered on and produced a book that I am so happy with! I am very grateful for your insights and support for my first book. Thank you for making my book better. 'The purpose of life is to contribute in some way to making things better'

Robert F. Kennedy

I am so grateful for ALL the love, support and wisdom of many many others who shine their support to me and this energises me to keep going. Thank you to all who have shared their laughter journey with me and supported my healing work. Your heartfelt stories have inspired me to spread my joyful services. I look forward to meeting you and serving many more. My wish is to continue to expand my laughter work far and wide. 'I live my life in widening circles, that reach out across the world'.

Rainer Maria Rilke

CHAPTER NOTES

INTRODUCTION

1. Cousins, N. (1976). Anatomy of an Illness (as Perceived by the Patient). N Engl J Med 1976; 295:1458–1463
2. Cousins, N. (2005) Anatomy of an Illness: As Perceived by the Patient (Twentieth Anniversary Edition. W. W. Norton & Company
3. Los Angeles Times (1990). The Positive Influence of Norman Cousins. Retrieved 23 January 2020 from: https://www.latimes.com/archives/la-xpm-1990-12-06-vw-8306-story.html

PART ONE

Welcome to Laugh More

1. Gable, S.L. & Haidt, J. (2005). What (and Why) Is Positive Psychology? Review of General Psychology. 9.
2. Fermelia, A. (2015). Beginning Thought Knowledge. Retrieved 23 March 2020 from: https://www.researchgate.net/publication/288503547_Beginning_Thought_Knowledge
3. Wood, K. (2013). The lost art of introspection: Why you must master yourself. Expert Enough. Retrieved 25 April 2020 from: http://expertenough.com/2990/the-lost-art-of-introspection-why-you-must-master-yourself
4. Norman, M. & Hyland, T. (2003). The Role of Confidence in Lifelong Learning. Educational Studies. 29. 261–272.
5. Diener, E & Sandvik, E & Pavot, W. (2009). Happiness is the Frequency, Not the Intensity, of Positive Versus Negative Affect. Diener, Ed. (2009). Assessing Well-Being: The Collected Works of Ed Diener. Springer.
6. Sin NL, Lyubomirsky S. (2009) Enhancing well-being and alleviating depressive symptoms with positive psychology interventions: a practice-friendly meta-analysis. J Clin Psychol. 2009;65(5):467–487.

7. Frates, E. & Louie, D. & Brooks, K. (2014). The Laughter Prescription: A Tool for Lifestyle Medicine. American Journal of Lifestyle Medicine. 10.

8. Lyubomirsky, S., & Layous, K. (2013). How Do Simple Positive Activities Increase Well-Being? Current Directions in Psychological Science, 22(1), 57–62.

Chapter 1 Why Laugh More?

1. Vale R. D. (2013). The value of asking questions. Molecular biology of the cell, 24(6), 680–68. Questions can act as a fast method for our brains to physically change (neuroplasticity) to encourage creative thinking and new knowledge. Asking good questions helps you to focus on what you want to do. With the insight that follows, you can move forward with clarity and commitment. When you ask a question, the entire brain gets active as it reflects. This encourages gathering intelligence from all areas of the brain, allowing for more insight. New brain connections begin to be made as the brain moves closer to finding solutions.

2. Berger, W. (2014) A More Beautiful Question: The Power of Inquiry to Spark Breakthrough Ideas. Bloomsbury USA

3. Garry, M., & Polaschek, D. L. L. (2000). Imagination and Memory. Current Directions in Psychological Science, 9(1), 6–10. Behaviours can be increased just by asking about them. Prompting the brain to contemplate a behaviour, increases that it will be acted upon.

4. Action for Happiness: 10 keys to happier living. Retrieved 9 February 2020 from: https://www.actionforhappiness.org/10-keys

5. Tabassum. F., Mohan J., & Smith P. Association of volunteering with mental well-being: a lifecourse analysis of a national population-based longitudinal study in the UK BMJ Open 2016; 6:e011327.

6. Du, S. & Martinez, A.M. Wait, are you sad or angry? Large exposure time differences required for the categorization of facial expressions of emotion. Journal of Vision 2013;13(4):13.

7. Wilkinson, A., Bowen, L., Gustavsson, E., Håkansson, S., Littleton, N., McCormick, J., Thompson, M., & Mulligan, H. (2019). Maintenance and Development of Social Connection by People with Long-term Conditions: A Qualitative Study. International journal of environmental research and public health, 16(11), 1875.

8. Kurtz, L. E., & Algoe, S. B. (2015). Putting Laughter in Context: Shared Laughter as Behavioral Indicator of Relationship Well-Being. Personal Relationships, 22(4), 573–590.

9. Yim, Jongeun. (2016). Therapeutic Benefits of Laughter in Mental Health: A Theoretical Review. The Tohoku Journal of Experimental Medicine. 239. 243-249.

10. Berk, Lee & Tan, Stanley & Berk, Dottie. (2008). Cortisol and Catecholamine stress hormone decrease is associated with the behavior of perceptual anticipation of mirthful laughter. The FASEB Journal. 22.

11. Han, Ji & Park, Kyung & Park, Heeok. (2017). Effects of Laughter Therapy on Depression and Sleep among Patients at Long-term Care Hospitals. Korean Journal of Adult Nursing. 29. 560–568.

12. Takeda, Masatoshi et al. 'Laughter and humor as complementary and alternative medicines for dementia patients.' BMC complementary and alternative medicine vol. 10 28. 18 Jun. 2010, doi:10.1186/1472-6882-10-28.

13. Martin, R.A. & Ford, T.E. (2018). The Clinical Psychology of Humor: Humor and Mental Health: An Integrative Approach. Cambridge, MA: Academic Press Publishing Company.

14. Fry, W. F. (1994). The biology of humor. Humor: International Journal of Humor Research, 7(2), 111–126. https://doi.org/10.1515/humr.1994.7.2.111.

15. Filippelli M, Pellegrino R, Iandelli I, et al. Respiratory dynamics during laughter. J Appl Physiol (1985). 2001;90(4):1441–1446.

16. American Heart Association, Humor helps your heart? How? accessed 8 October 2019: http://www.heart.org/HEARTORG/Conditions/More/MyHeartandStrokeNews/Humor-helps-your-heart-How_UCM_447039_Article.jsp#.XZyL50ZKjDc

17. Pérez-Aranda, A., Hofmann, J., Feliu-Soler, A., Ramírez-Maestre, C., Andrés-Rodríguez, L., Ruch, W. & Luciano, J.V. (2019). Laughing away the pain: A narrative review of humour, sense of humour and pain. European Journal of Pain, 23 (2), 220–233.

18. Association for Applied and Therapeutic Humor: https://www.aath.org/

19. The Chopra Center. Laughter Meditation: 5 Healing Benefits and a 10-Minute Practice. Retrieved 19 February 2020 from: https://chopra.com/articles/laughter-meditation-5-healing-benefits-and-a-10-minute-practice

20. Edutopia, Laughter and Learning: Humor Boosts Retention Retrieved 22 February 2020 from: https://www.edutopia.org/blog/laughter-learning-humor-boosts-retention-sarah-henderson

21. Kuiper, Nicholas. (2012). Humor and Resiliency: Towards a Process Model of Coping and Growth. Europe's Journal of Psychology. 8. 475–491.

22. Newport Academy. Why Laughter Is Good for Mental Health. Retrieved 22 February 2020 from: https://www.newportacademy.com/resources/mental-health/laughter-good-for-you/

23. Cohn, M.A. & Fredrickson, B.L.. (2012). Positive Emotions. Oxford handbook of positive psychology. 13–24.

24. Hofmann, Jennifer & Platt, Tracey & Ruch, Willibald. (2017). Laughter and Smiling in 16 Positive Emotions. IEEE Transactions on Affective Computing. PP. 1–1.

25. Yim, Jongeun. (2016). Therapeutic Benefits of Laughter in Mental Health: A Theoretical Review. The Tohoku Journal of Experimental Medicine. 239. 243–249.

26. Bitterly, T. & Brooks, A. & Schweitzer, M. (2016). Risky Business: When Humor Increases and Decreases Status. Journal of Personality and Social Psychology. 112.

Chapter 2 What is Laughter and How You Can Make it a Choice

1. Savage, B. & Lujan, H.& Thipparthi, R. & Dicarlo, S. (2017). Humor, laughter, learning, and health! A brief review. Advances in Physiology Education. 41. 341–347.
2. M & Wilson, D. S. (2006). The evolution and functions of laughter and humor: A synthetic approach. The Quarterly review of biology. 80. 395–430.
3. Butler, B. (2005). Laughter: The Best Medicine?. OLA Quarterly. 11. 11–13.
4. Wilkins, J. & Eisenbraun, A. (2009). Humor theories and the physiological benefits of laughter. Advances in mind-body medicine. 24. 8–12.
5. Nelson, J.. (2007). Laugh and the World Laughs with You: An Attachment Perspective on the Meaning of Laughter in Psychotherapy. Clinical Social Work Journal. 36. 41–49.
6. Erickson, D & Menezes, C. & Sakakibara, K. (2009). Are you laughing, smiling or crying?. APSIPA ASC 2009 - Asia-Pacific Signal and Information Processing Association 2009 Annual Summit and Conference.
7. Provine, R. (2000). Laughter: A Scientific Investigation. Retrieved 6 May 2020 from: https://www.researchgate.net/publication/232489851_Laughter_A_Scientific_Investigation
8. Bennett, M. & Lengacher, C. (2006). Humor and Laughter may Influence Health. I. History and Background. Evidence-based complementary and alternative medicine : eCAM. 3. 61-3. 10.1093/ecam/nek015.
9. Laughter Yoga International : https://laughteryoga.org/
10. AEON. Knight, C. (2019) Did laughter make the mind? Retrieved 6 January 2020 from: https://aeon.co/essays/does-laughter-hold-the-key-to-human-consciousness
11. Meyer, M. & Baumann, S. & Wildgruber, D. & Alter, K. (2007). How the brain laughs. Behavioural brain research. 182. 245–60.
12. Scott, S. & Lavan, N. & Chen, S. & Mcgettigan, C. (2014). The social life of laughter. Trends in cognitive sciences. 18.
13. Gordon, J.S.: https://cmbm.org/about/founder/
14. Zajenkowski, M. & Jankowski, K.& Kołata, D. (2015). Let's dance - feel better! Mood changes following dancing in different situations. European Journal of Sport Science. 15. 640–646.
15. Penton-Voak, I. S., Thomas, J., Gage, S. H., McMurran, M., McDonald, S., & Munafò, M. R. (2013). Increasing Recognition of Happiness in Ambiguous Facial Expressions Reduces Anger and Aggressive Behavior. Psychological Science, 24(5), 688–697.
16. Matthews, G Goals research summary Retrieved May 2, 2020 from http://www.goalband.co.uk/uploads/1/0/6/5/10653372/gail_matthews_research_summary.pdf http://www.goalband.co.uk/uploads/1/0/6/5/10653372/about_gail_matthews_ph_d.pdf http://www.goalband.co.uk/uploads/1/0/6/5/10653372/strategies_for_achieving_goals_gail_matthews_dominican_university_of_california.pdf
17. Hussain, D. (2010). Healing Through Writing: Insights from Research. The International Journal of Mental Health Promotion. 12. 19-23.

Chapter 3 Start your Laughter with a Smile

1. Krämer, N. & Kopp, S. & Sommer, N. & Becker-Asano, C. (2009). Smile and the world will smile with you - The effects of a virtual agent's smile on users' evaluation and non-conscious behavioral mimicry. International Journal of Human-Computer Studies.
2. Hofmann, J. & Platt, T. & Ruch, W. (2017). Laughter and Smiling in 16 Positive Emotions. IEEE Transactions on Affective Computing. PP. 1–1.
3. Chapell, M. S. (1997). Frequency of Public Smiling across the Life Span. Perceptual and Motor Skills, 85(3_suppl), 1326–1326. https://doi.org/10.2466/pms.1997.85.3f.1326
4. Navarretta, C. (2016). Mirroring Facial Expressions and Emotions in Dyadic Conversations. Conference: Language Resources and Evaluation Conference (LREC 2016), At Portoroz, Slovenia, Volume: 10.
5. John, Daniel. (2019). The Impact of Smile on Human Interactions: A Psychological Perspective. The International Journal of Indian Psychology 7(1).
6. Campbell, S (2004) Watch Me Grow! A Unique, 3-Dimensional Week-by-Week Look at Your Baby's Behaviour and Development in the Womb. Carroll & Brown.
7. Niedenthal, P. (2018). Reinforcing, Reassuring, and Roasting: The Forms and Functions of the Human Smile. ICMI '18: Proceedings of the 20th ACM International Conference on Multimodal Interaction. 3-3.
8. Beamish, A & Olbers, T.& Foster, J. & Edwards, H.. (2019). What's in a smile? A review of the benefits of the clinician's smile. Postgraduate medical journal.
9. Dfarhud, D & Malmir, M. & Khanahmadi, M. (2014). Happiness & Health: The Biological Factors- Systematic Review Article. Iranian journal of public health. 43. 1468–77.
10. Korb, S., With, S.,Niedenthal, P.,Kaiser, S., & Grandjean, D. (2014). The Perception and Mimicry of Facial Movements Predict Judgments of Smile Authenticity. PloS one. 9. e99194.
11. Williams, L., Senior, C., David, A., Loughland, C., & Gordon, E. (2001). In Search of the Duchenne Smile: Evidence from Eye Movements. Journal of Psychophysiology - J PSYCHOPHYSIOL. 15. 122–127.
12. Hertenstein, Matthew & Hansel, Carrie & Butts, Alissa & Hile, Sarah. (2009). Smile intensity in photographs predicts divorce later in life. Motivation and Emotion. 33. 99–105.
13. Aoun, M., Sleilaty, G., Antoun, L., Dib, R., & Chelala, D. (2020). Duchenne Smile is Associated with Quality of Life and Survival in Hemodialysis Patients. American journal of health behavior. 44. 313–325. 10.5993/AJHB.44.3.4.
14. Abel, Ernest & Kruger, Michael. (2010). Smile Intensity in Photographs Predicts Longevity. Psychological science. 21. 542–4.
15. Girard, J., Shandar, G., Liu, Z. Cohn, J., Yin, L. & Morency, L. (2019). Reconsidering the Duchenne Smile: Indicator of Positive Emotion or Artifact of Smile Intensity?. International Conference on Affective Computing and Intelligent Interaction and workshops : [proceedings]. ACII (Conference). 2019. 594–599.
16. Bogodistov, Y & Dost, F. (2017). Proximity Begins with a Smile, But Which One? Associating Non-duchenne Smiles with Higher Psychological Distance. Frontiers in Psychology. 8. 1374. 10.3389/fpsyg.2017.01374.

17. Messinger, D.S & Fogel, A. & Dickson, K.L. 'What's in a Smile?', Developmental Psychology, 35 (1999), 701–08.

18. Messinger, D.S & Fogel, A. & Dickson, K.L. 'All Smiles are Positive, but Some Smiles are More Positive than Others', Developmental Psychology, 37, 5 (2001), 642–653.

19. Fogel, A. & Nelson-Goens, G. & Hsu, H. (2000). Do Different Infant Smiles Reflect Different Positive Emotions?. Social Development. 9. 497–520.

20. Mehu, M. & Little, A, & Dunbar, R. (2007). Duchenne smiles and the perception of generosity and sociability in faces. Journal of Evolutionary Psychology. 5. 133–146.

21. Hayward, D., Pereira, E., Otto, A. & Ristic, J. (2018). Smile! Social Reward Drives Attention. Journal of Experimental Psychology Human Perception & Performance. 44. 206–214.

22. Yagil,D. & Medler-liraz, H. (2016). Personally Committed to Emotional Labor: Surface Acting, Emotional Exhaustion and Performance Among Service Employees With a Strong Need to Belong. Journal of occupational health psychology. 22. 10.1037/ocp0000049.

23. Wheelwright, S & Dickinson, C. & Pile, V. & Seleznev, A. & Baron-Cohen, S. (2009). Can People with Asperger Syndrome Identify Fake Smiles?. Conference: International Meeting for Autism Research 2009.

24. The Guardian. (2015) Psychology of smiling: can you tell a fake smile from a genuine one?. Retrieved 23 February 2020 from: https://www.theguardian.com/science/2015/apr/10/psychology-empathy-distinguish-fake-genuine-smiles

25. Gunnery, S., Hall, J & Ruben, M. (2012). The Deliberate Duchenne Smile: Individual Differences in Expressive Control. Journal of Nonverbal Behavior. 37.

26. Vittorio G. (2009) Mirror Neurons, Embodied Simulation, and the Neural Basis of Social Identification, Psychoanalytic Dialogues, 19:5, 519–536.

27. Ramachandran, V. Reflecting on the mind. Nature 452, 814–815 (2008).

28. The Mirror Neuron Revolution: Explaining What Makes Humans Social. Retrieved 23 February 2020 from: https://www.scientificamerican.com/article/the-mirror-neuron-revolut/

29. Arapova, M.A. (2017) Cultural differences in Russian and Western smiling, Russian Journal of Communication, 9:1, 34–52.

30. The Conversation. (2018). Why are Russians so stingy with their smiles? Retrieved 23 March 2020 from: https://theconversation.com/why-are-russians-so-stingy-with-their-smiles-98799

31. Gartstein, M.A., Knyazev, G.G. & Slobodskaya, H.R. Cross-cultural differences in the structure of infant temperament: United States of America (US) and Russia. Infant Behavior and Development, 2005, 28(1) 54–61

32. Gartstein, M.A., Slobodskaya, H.R., Putnam, S.P. &. Kinsht, I.A (2009) A cross-cultural study of infant temperament: Predicting preschool effortful control in the United States of America and Russia, European Journal of Developmental Psychology, 6:3, 337–364,

Chapter 4 Your Unique Laugh

1. Bryant, G. A., Fessler, D. M. T., Fusaroli, R., Clint, E., Amir, D., Chávez, B., ... Zhou, Y. (2018). The Perception of Spontaneous and Volitional Laughter Across 21 Societies. Psychological Science, 29(9), 1515–1525.
2. Manninen S, Tuominen L, Dunbar RI, et al. Social Laughter Triggers Endogenous Opioid Release in Humans. J Neurosci. 2017;37(25):6125–6131.
3. Bennett, Mary P., "Humor Response Scale" (2003). Nursing Faculty Publications. Paper 10. http://digitalcommons.wku.edu/nurs_fac_pub/10
4. Bennett, Mary P.; Zeller, Janice M.; Rosenberg, Lisa; and McCann, Judith. (2003). The Effect of Mirthful Laughter on Stress and Natural Killer Cell Activity. Alternative Therapies in Health and Medicine, 9 (2), 38–45.
5. Bachorowski, J., Smoski. M.J. & Owren, M.J.(2001) The acoustic features of human laughter. The Journal of the Acoustical Society of America 110, 1581
6. UMBC News, Robert Provine, Psychology, in Vox and on Today.com Retrieved 6 February 2020 from: https://news.umbc.edu/robert-provine-psychology-in-vox-and-on-today-com/
7. Scientific American. Why can't a person tickle himself? Retrieved 7 February 2020 from: https://www.scientificamerican.com/article/why-cant-a-person-tickle/
8. Turnbull, Colin M. 1962. The Forest People. New York: Simon and Schuster
9. O'Hanlon, R. (1987) Into the Heart of Borneo (Vintage). The story of a 1983 journey to the centre of Borneo, which no expedition had attempted since 1926. O'Hanlon, accompanied by friend and poet James Fenton and three native guides, brings wit and humour to a dangerous journey. The humour throughout the book is strong and does not spare anyone, including the author himself. Misadventures described with high humour.
10. Association for Psychological Science (2018) Ability to Identify Genuine Laughter Transcends Culture. Retrieved 7 February 2020 from: https://www.psychologicalscience.org/news/releases/ability-to-identify-genuine-laughter-transcends-culture.html
11. VICE. Psychology. Experts Explain Why You Laugh When You Shouldn't. Retrieved 7 February 2020 from: https://www.vice.com/en_uk/article/yw55yw/experts-explain-why-you-laugh-when-you-shouldnt
12. Greater Good Science Center (GGSC). How Laughter Brings Us Together Retrieved 7 February 2020 from: https://greatergood.berkeley.edu/article/item/how_laughter_brings_us_together
13. Brown, B. (2007). I Thought It Was Just Me (but it isn't): Making the Journey from "What Will People Think?" to "I Am Enough. Avery.
14. Brown, Brene TedTalk https://www.ted.com/talks/brene_brown_the_power_of_vulnerability?language=en
15. Cancer Treatment Centers of America (CTCA). (2019) The power of laughter for cancer patients. Retrieved 17 February 2020 from: https://www.cancercenter.com/community/blog/2019/12/power-of-laughter-for-cancer-patients
16. The Association for Applied and Therapeutic Humor: https://www.aath.org/
17. Dunbar, R. I., Baron, R., Frangou, A., Pearce, E., van Leeuwen, E. J., Stow, J., Partridge, G., MacDonald, I., Barra, V., & van Vugt, M. (2012). Social laughter

is correlated with an elevated pain threshold. Proceedings. Biological sciences, 279(1731), 1161–1167.

18. ABC Science. Humour in medical setting can backfire-study. Retrieved 21 February 2020 from https://www.abc.net.au/science/articles/2003/07/01/891200.htm
19. Laughter Yoga International : https://laughteryoga.org/
20. Farifteh, S., Mohammadi-Aria, A., Kiamanesh, A., & Mofid, B. (2014). The Impact of Laughter Yoga on the Stress of Cancer Patients before Chemotherapy. Iranian journal of cancer prevention, 7(4), 179–183.
21. The U.S. National Cancer Institute (NCI) produces the NCI Dictionary of Cancer Terms. Retrieved 17 February 2020 from: https://www.cancer.gov/publications/dictionaries/cancer-terms/def/laughter-therapy
22. Wanzer M, Booth-Butterfield M, Booth-Butterfield S. "If we didn't use humor, we'd cry": humorous coping communication in health care settings. J Health Commun. 2005;10(2):105–125.
23. The ASCO Post. (2019) Laughter in Oncology Is More Common Than You Think Retrieved 27 February 2020 from: https://www.ascopost.com/issues/july-25-2019/laughter-in-oncology-is-more-common-than-you-think/

Chapter 5 Laughter and Play

1. Brown. S. (2010) Play: How It Shapes the Brain, Opens the Imagination, and Invigorates the Soul. J P Tarcher/Penguin Putnam Reprint edition.
2. Fredrickson B. L. (2004). The broaden-and-build theory of positive emotions. Philosophical transactions of the Royal Society of London. Series B, Biological sciences, 359(1449), 1367–1378.
3. Stanford Encyclopedia of Philosophy (2012) Philosophy of Humor. Retrieved 21 January 2020 from: https://plato.stanford.edu/entries/humor/
4. Winerman. L. (2006). A laughing matter. Psychologists are finding that the ancient roots of laughter predate the idea of "funny". American Psychological Association 37(7) 58.
5. Shuster S. (2007) Sex, aggression, and humour: responses to unicycling BMJ 2007; 335 :1320.
6. Testosterone is the main male steroid hormone, driving the development of male sex characteristics. It's typically considered the prime hormonal driver of anabolism, the process by which things grow – particularly muscle. While testosterone is primarily a masculine hormone, females do also possess it, just at far lower levels than men. This is one of the main reasons why females tend to have less muscle mass than their male counterparts.
7. Retrieved 17 February 2020 from: https://dictionary.cambridge.org/dictionary/english/play, https://www.dictionary.com/browse/play https://www.vocabulary.com/dictionary/play
8. Magnuson, C & Barnett, L. (2013). The Playful Advantage: How Playfulness Enhances Coping with Stress. Leisure Sciences. 35. 129–144.
9. ANNE ARUNDEL MEDICAL CENTER (2019) The Benefits of Play for Adults Retrieved 17 February 2020 from https://living.aahs.org/behavioral-health/the-benefits-of-play-for-adults/

10. Brown. S. (2010) Play: How It Shapes the Brain, Opens the Imagination, and Invigorates the Soul. J P Tarcher/Penguin Putnam Reprint edition.
11. Brown. S. (2008) TEDTALKS. Play is more than just fun https://www.ted.com/talks/stuart_brown_play_is_more_than_just_fun/transcript?language=en
12. Time devoted to unstructured children's play for many children in the UK and America has been reduced. Changes that have contributed to this are adult-directed activities, extended school days, overemphasis on academic achievement and parental fear for child safety. Also, a move from informal, natural play spaces to explore to standard playgrounds, play within the home and a shift from homemade and improvised toys to educational, manufactured, and electronic choices.
13. Duckworth, A (2016). Grit: The Power of Passion and Perseverance Scribner Book Company.

Chapter 6 Laughing with Others

1. Provine R.R.Contagious laughter—laughter is a sufficient stimulus for laughs and smiles. Bull. Psychon. Soc. 1992; 30: 1–4.
2. Martin, R. A., & Kuiper, N. A. (1999). Daily occurrence of laughter: Relationships with age, gender, and Type A personality. Humor: International Journal of Humor Research, 12(4), 355–384.
3. Provine, R. R., & Fischer, K. R. (1989). Laughing, smiling, and talking: Relation to sleeping and social context in humans. Ethology, 83(4), 295–305.
4. Bainum, C. K., Lounsbury, K. R., & Pollio, H. R. (1984). The development of laughing and smiling in nursery school children. Child Development, 55(5), 1946–1957.
5. Nwokah, E. E., Hsu, H.-C., Dobrowolska, O., & Fogel, A. (1994). The development of laughter in mother-infant communication: Timing parameters and temporal sequences. Infant Behavior & Development, 17(1), 23–35.
6. Brewer, K. (2018). Don't Make Me Laugh!: Morality, Ethics, and the Laugh Track. Studies in American Humor, 4(1), 10–36.
7. Cai Q, Chen S, White SJ, Scott SK. Modulation of humor ratings of bad jokes by other people's laughter. Curr Biol. 2019;29(14):R677–R678.
8. Pang, D., & Proyer, R. T. (2018). An Initial Cross-Cultural Comparison of Adult Playfulness in Mainland China and German-Speaking Countries. Frontiers in psychology, 9, 421.
9. Proyer, R.T. (2017). A new structural model for the study of adult playfulness: Assessment and exploration of an understudied individual differences variable. Personality and Individual Differences, 108, 113–122.
10. Proyer, R. T., Gander, F., Bertenshaw, E. J., & Brauer, K. (2018). The Positive Relationships of Playfulness With Indicators of Health, Activity, and Physical Fitness. Frontiers in psychology, 9, 1440.
11. Strean W. B. (2009). Laughter prescription. Canadian family physician Medecin de famille canadien, 55(10), 965–967.
12. Bryant. G.A, & Aktipis. C.A.(2014).The animal nature of spontaneous human laughter. Evolution and Human Behavior. 35 (4), 327–335.

13. Bryant, G. A., Fessler, D. M. T., Fusaroli, R., Clint, E., Amir, D., Chávez, B., ... Zhou, Y. (2018). The Perception of Spontaneous and Volitional Laughter Across 21 Societies. Psychological Science, 29(9), 1515–1525.

14. Relevant. (2016) You Can Actually Tell When Your Friends Are Fake Laughing at Your Jokes, Because Science. Retrieved 26 March 2020, from: https://relevantmagazine.com/culture/you-can-actually-tell-when-your-friends-are-fake-laughing-your-jokes-because-science/

15. The New York Times. (2016) The Fake Laugh Retrieved 16 March 2020 https://www.nytimes.com/2016/10/23/opinion/sunday/the-science-of-the-fake-laugh.html

16. Ferguson, Mark & Ford, Thomas. (2008). Disparagement humor: A theoretical and empirical review of psychoanalytic, superiority, and social identity theories. Humor-international Journal of Humor Research - HUMOR. 21. 283–312.

17. Thomas, Emma & McGarty, Craig & Spears, Russell & Livingstone, Andrew & Platow, Michael & Lala, Girish & Mavor, Ken. (2020). 'That's not funny!' Standing up against disparaging humor. Journal of Experimental Social Psychology. 86. 103901.

18. Tomasello M. (2014). The ultra-social animal. European journal of social psychology, 44(3), 187–194.

19. Post, S.G. Altruism, happiness, and health: it's good to be good. Int. J. Behav. Med. 12, 66–77 (2005).

20. Oarga, Cristina & Stavrova, Olga & Fetchenhauer, Detlef. (2014). When and why is helping others good for well-being? The role of belief in reciprocity and conformity to society's expectations. European Journal of Social Psychology. 45.

Chapter 7 Making Laughter a Daily Habit

1. Smith, K. S., & Graybiel, A. M. (2016). Habit formation. Dialogues in clinical neuroscience, 18(1), 33–43.

2. Society for Personality and Social Psychology. (2014, August 8). How we form habits, change existing ones. ScienceDaily. Retrieved March 28, 2020 from www.sciencedaily.com/releases/2014/08/140808111931.htm

3. Duke Today. (2007). Key to changing habits is in environment, not willpower, Duke expert says. Retrieved March 28, 2020 from https://today.duke.edu/2007/12/habit.html

4. Neal, David & Wood, Wendy & Labrecque, Jennifer & Lally, Phillippa. (2012). How do habits guide behavior? Perceived and actual triggers of habits in daily life. Journal of Experimental Social Psychology. 48. 492–498.

5. Neal, D. T., Wood, W., & Quinn, J. M. (2006). Habits—A Repeat Performance. Current Directions in Psychological Science, 15(4), 198–202.

6. Lally, P. & Jaarsveld, C. & Potts, H. & Wardle, J. (2010). How are habits formed: Modeling habit formation in the real world. European Journal of Social Psychology. 40(6).

7. Matthews, G Goals research summary Retrieved May 2, 2020 from http://www.goalband.co.uk/uploads/1/0/6/5/10653372/gail_matthews_research_summary.pdf http://www.goalband.co.uk/uploads/1/0/6/5/10653372/about_gail_matthews_ph_d.pdf http://www.goalband.co.uk/uploads/1/0/6/5/10653372/strategies_for_achieving_goals_gail_matthews_dominican_university_of_california.pdf

8. Just saying trigger snigger makes me laugh Snigger is a common word in the UK and means to laugh in a silly way, and is suppressed laughter. The word 'snigger' reminds me of growing up and hearing Muttley a fictional dog, who was the comic foil to the cartoon villain Dick Dastardly, in the 1968 television series Wacky Races. The character is known best for his mischievous laughter.

9. Matthews, G Goals research summary Retrieved May 2, 2020 from: http://www.goalband.co.uk/uploads/1/0/6/5/10653372/strategies_for_achieving_goals_gail_matthews_dominican_university_of_california.pdf

10. Sansone, R. A., & Sansone, L. A. (2010). Gratitude and well being: the benefits of appreciation. Psychiatry (Edgmont) 7(11), 18–22.

11. Greater Good Science Center.(2010) Why Gratitude Is Good. Retrieved March 12, 2020 from: https://greatergood.berkeley.edu/article/item/why_gratitude_is_good

12. Emmons, R.A., McCullough M. E., (2003). Counting Blessings Versus Burdens: An Experimental Investigation of Gratitude and Subjective Well-Being in Daily Life. Journal of Personality and Social Psychology 84(2), 377–389.

13. Wood A.M, Joseph S, Lloyd J, Atkins S (2009). Gratitude influences sleep through the mechanism of pre-sleep cognitions. Journal of Psychosomatic Research, 66(1):43–8.

Chapter 8 Laughter, Workplace Performance and More

1. TALBOT, LAURA & LUMDEN, D.. (2000). On the association between humor and burnout. Humor-international Journal of Humor Research - HUMOR. 13. 419–428.

2. Baas, Matthijs & De Dreu, Carsten & Nijstad, Bernard. (2008). A Meta-Analysis of 25 Years of Mood-Creativity Research: Hedonic Tone, Activation, or Regulatory Focus?. Psychological bulletin. 134. 779–806.

3. Warren, J.E. (2006). Positive Emotions Preferentially Engage an Auditory-Motor "Mirror" System. The Journal of Neuroscience. 26 (50) 13067–13075

4. Kurtz, L. E., & Algoe, S. B. (2015). Putting Laughter in Context: Shared Laughter as Behavioral Indicator of Relationship Well-Being. Personal Relationships, 22(4), 573–590.

5. Vetter, Laura & Gockel, Christine. (2016). Can't buy me laughter – Humour in organisational change. Gruppe. Interaktion. Organisation. Zeitschrift für Angewandte Organisationspsychologie (GIO). 47.

6. Gunnery, S.D., Hall, J.A. The Duchenne Smile and Persuasion. J Nonverbal Behav 38, 181–194 (2014).

7. Scott. B.A, Barnes. C.C & Wagner D.A. Chameleonic or consistent? a multilevel investigation of emotional labor variability and self-monitoringThe Academy of Management Journal Vol. 55, No. 4 (August 2012), pp. 905–926.

8. Apte, M.L. (1985) Humor and Laughter: An Anthropological Approach. Cornell University Press.

9. Johnson, J.C, Boster, J.S. & Palinkas, L.A. The Evolution of Networks in Extreme and Isolated Environments Retrieved Feb 2, 2020 from: https://ntrs.nasa.gov/archive/nasa/casi.ntrs.nasa.gov/20000062463.pdf

10. Oswald, A.J., Proto,E. & Sgroi, D. 'Happiness and Productivity', Journal of Labor Economics 33, no. 4 (October 2015): 789–822.

11. Inc. (2018) Here's the Only Definition of Leadership That Matters. Retrieved May 21, 2020 from: https://www.inc.com/john-brandon/heres-only-definition-of-leadership-that-matters.html
12. Oveis, C., Spectre, A., Smith, P.K., Liu, M.L. & Keltner, D. (2016). Laughter conveys status. Journal of Experimental Social Psychology. 65 (2016) 109–115.
13. Holmes, J & Marra, M. (2006). Humor and Leadership Style. Humor-international Journal of Humor Research - HUMOR. 19. 119–138. Bitterly, T. & Brooks, Alison & Schweitzer, Maurice. (2016). Risky Business: When Humor Increases and Decreases Status. Journal of Personality and Social Psychology 112(3), 431–455.
14. Hayati, D., Charkhabi, M., & Naami, A. (2014). The relationship between transformational leadership and work engagement in governmental hospitals nurses: a survey study. SpringerPlus, 3, 25.
15. Pundt, A., & Herrmann, F. (2015). Affiliative and aggressive humour in leadership and their relationship to leader-member exchange. Journal Of Occupational & Organizational Psychology, 88(1), 108–125.
16. Tremblay, M., & Gibson, M. (2016). The Role of Humor in the Relationship Between Transactional Leadership Behavior, Perceived Supervisor Support, and Citizenship Behavior. Journal Of Leadership And Organizational Studies, 23(1), 39–54.
17. Hoption, C., Barling, J., & Turner, N. (2013). "It's not you, it's me": transformational leadership and self deprecating humor. Leadership & Organization Development Journal, 34(1), 4–19.
18. Bitterly, T. & Brooks, Alison & Schweitzer, Maurice. (2016). Risky Business: When Humor Increases and Decreases Status. Journal of Personality and Social Psychology. 112.
19. American Psychological Association. Teaching Tip Sheet: Self-Efficacy. Retrieved May 21, 2020 from: https://www.apa.org/pi/aids/resources/education/self-efficacy
20. Bandura, A. (1997). Self-efficacy. The exercise of control. New York: W. H. Freeman and Company.
21. Beckman, H., Regier, N., & Young, J. (2007). Effect of workplace laughter groups on personal efficacy beliefs. The Journal of Primary Prevention, 28, 167–182.
22. Sims, P. (2011) Little Bets, How Breakthrough Ideas Emerge from Small Discoveries. Simon & Schuster; Reprint edition.
23. Acar, S. & Runco, M.A (2012) Creative Abilities: Divergent Thinking, Handbook of Organizational Creativity, Academic Press, 6, 115–139.
24. Goleman, D. J. (1995) Emotional Intelligence:84–86 Bantam Books.
25. Powell, J.P & Andresen, L.W. (1985) Humour and teaching in higher education, Studies in Higher Education, 10:1, 79–90.
26. Carlson, K. (2011). The impact of humor on memory: Is the humor effect about humor?. Humor - International Journal of Humor Research. 24.
27. samrehan.com
28. Landon LB, Slack KJ, Barrett JD. Teamwork and collaboration in long-duration space missions: Going to extremes. Am Psychol. 2018;73(4):563–575.
29. Laughter Yoga International: https://laughteryoga.org/

Chapter 9 Happy Ageing

1. Rowe, J.W. & Kahn R.L. (1999) Successful Aging. Dell Describes successful ageing as "multidimensional, encompassing the avoidance of disease and disability, the maintenance of high physical and cognitive function, and sustained engagement in social and productive activities."
2. Bowling, A. & Dieppe, P. (2005) What is successful ageing and who should define it? BMJ. 2005 Dec 24; 331(7531): 1548–1551.
3. Solomon, J. C. (1996). Humor and aging well: A laughing matter or a matter of laughing? American Behavioral Scientist, 39(3), 249–271.
4. Jeanne Calment and her successors. Biographical notes on the longest living humans. Retrieved 26 March 2020, from https://www.demogr.mpg.de/books/drm/007/3-4.pdf
5. Scelzo, A., Di Somma, S., Antonini, P., Montross, L., Schork, N., Brenner, D., & Jeste, D. (2018). Mixed-methods quantitative–qualitative study of 29 nonagenarians and centenarians in rural Southern Italy: Focus on positive psychological traits. International Psychogeriatrics, 30(1), 31–38.
6. Friedman, H.S. (2012). The Longevity Project: Surprising Discoveries for Health and Long Life from the Landmark Eight-Decade Study. Plume.
7. Greene, C.M., Morgan, J.C., LaVona S., Traywick, L.S., & Mingo, C.A. (2017). Evaluation of a Laughter-based Exercise Program on Health and Self-efficacy for Exercise. Gerontologist, 57, 6, 1051–1061. Participants reported that 96.2% found laughter to be an enjoyable addition to a traditional exercise programme, 88.9% said laughter helped make exercise more accessible and 88.9% reported the programme enhanced their motivation to participate in other exercise classes.
8. Havighurst, R.J., Successful Aging, The Gerontologist, Volume 1, Issue 1, March 1961, Pages 8–13. The phrase 'Successful Ageing' was introduced by Robert Havighurst in 1961 at a time when Cumming & Henry's (1961) "Disengagement Theory" was popular. Disengagement theory talked about ageing naturally involved an inevitable and progressive withdrawal from social institutions and loss of the individual. In contrast, Havighurst's Activity Theory proposed that late life involves maintenance and replacement of the activities and attitudes of middle age. Rather than withdrawing from activities, Havighurst advocated for engagement in new social roles such as grandparenting.
9. I facilitated seated laughter yoga with groups of residential clients, in various care homes. Many clients were diagnosed with dementia. With those with severe dementia, the care workers present verbally reported surprise and astonishment when laughter group activities raised speech and enjoyment. In one care home, I was told that it was unlikely that residents would participate because of the very little engagement normally shown. In this session, one by one I knelt, offered my hand and looked into the client's eyes as I smiled warmly. I laughed gently and, in most cases, a smile or laugh would be offered back. The individual attention and touch seem to facilitate the expression of happiness.
10. Manninen, S., Tuominen, L., Dunbar, R., Karjalainen, T., Hirvonen, J., Arponen, E., Hari, R., Jääskeläinen, I.P., Sams, M. & Nummenma, L (June 2017). Social Laughter Triggers Endogenous Opioid Release in Humans. Journal of Neuroscience 37 (25) 6125–6131.
11. James, B. D., Wilson, R. S., Barnes, L. L., & Bennett, D. A. (2011). Late-life social activity and cognitive decline in old age. Journal of the International Neuropsychological Society: JINS, 17(6), 998–1005.

12. Chopik WJ. The Benefits of Social Technology Use Among Older Adults Are Mediated by Reduced Loneliness. Cyberpsychol Behav Soc Netw. 2016;19(9):551–556.

13. Campos, B., Schoebi, D., Gonzaga, G.C., Gable S.L., & • Keltner D. (2015) Attuned to the positive? Awareness and responsiveness to others' positive emotion experience and display Motiv Emot (2015) 39:780–794.

14. Thompson, W., Roe C., Aspinall, J., Mitchell P,, Clow R., & Miller D. More green space is linked to less stress in deprived communities: Evidence from salivary cortisol patterns. Landscape and Urban Planning, Vol. 105, No. 3, 15.04.2012, p. 221–229.

15. Grinde B, Patil GG. (2009) Biophilia: does visual contact with nature impact on health and well-being?. Int J Environ Res Public Health. 6(9):2332–2343.

16. Aspinall, P., Mavros, P., Coyne, R., & Roe, J. The urban brain: analysing outdoor physical activity with mobile EEG. Br J Sports Med. 2015 Feb;49(4):272–6.

17. Engemann, K., Pedersen,C., Arge, L. Tsirogiannis, C. Mortensen, P & Svenning, J. Residential green space in childhood is associated with lower risk of psychiatric disorders from adolescence into adulthood. Proceedings of the National Academy of Sciences Mar 2019, 116 (11) 5188–5193.

18. White, M.P., Alcock, I., Grellier J., Wheeler B.W., Hartig T., Warber S.L., Bone A., Depledge M.H., Fleming L. E. (2019) Spending at least 120 minutes a week in nature is associated with good health and wellbeing. Sci Rep 9, 7730.

19. Keltner, D., Bowman R., and Richards H. (2017). University of Berkeley, California; BBC Worldwide Global Insight Team. Exploring the Emotional State of 'Real Happiness'. a Study into the Effects of Watching Natural History Television Content. Retrieved 26 March 2020, from https://asset-manager.bbcchannels.com/workspace/uploads/bbcw-real-happiness-white-paper-final-v2-58ac1df7.pdf

20. Toyoda. M., Yokota. Y., Barnes M. & Midori Kaneko (2019) Potential of a Small Indoor Plant on the Desk for Reducing Office Workers' Stress. HortTechnology 30 (1) 55–63.

21. Van den Berg MM, Maas J, Muller R. (2015) Autonomic Nervous System Responses to Viewing Green and Built Settings: Differentiating Between Sympathetic and Parasympathetic Activity. Int J Environ Res Public Health.;12(12):15860–15874.

22. Finlay J., Franke T., McKay H., Sims-Gould, J. (2015). Therapeutic landscapes and wellbeing in later life: Impacts of blue and green spaces for older adults. Health & Place, 2015; 34: 97.

23. MacKerron G. & Mourato S. (2013). Happiness is greater in natural environments. Global Environmental Change 23(5) 992–1000.

24. Cracknell D., White M.P., Wallace S.P., Nichols J., &. Depledge M.H Marine Biota and Psychological Well-Being: A Preliminary Examination of Dose–Response Effects in an Aquarium Setting. Environment and Behavior 2016, Vol. 48(10) 1242–1269.

25. Sheldon, K. M., & Lyubomirsky, S. (2006). How to increase and sustain positive emotion: The effects of expressing gratitude and visualizing best possible selves. The Journal of Positive Psychology, 1(2), 73–82.

26. Dossey, L (2018) The Helper's High. Explore (NY) 14(6):393–399.

27. Harris, A & Thoresen, C. (2005). Volunteering is Associated with Delayed Mortality in Older People: Analysis of the Longitudinal Study of Aging. Journal of Health Psychology. 10. 739–52.

28. Wood A.M., Froh J.J. & Geraghty A.W.A. (2010) Gratitude and Well-Being: A Review and Theoretical Integration Clinical Psychology Review. 30(7):890–905.

29. Ryan, R & Deci, E. (2001). On Happiness and Human Potentials: A Review of Research on Hedonic and Eudaimonic Well-Being. Annual review of psychology. 52. 141–66.

30. What Is Mindfulness? Retrieved 26 April 2020, from https://greatergood.berkeley.edu/topic/mindfulness/definition

31. Seear, K. & Vella-Brodrick, D. (2013). Efficacy of Positive Psychology Interventions to Increase Well-Being: Examining the Role of Dispositional Mindfulness. Social Indicators Research. 114.

32. Sin, Nancy & Lyubomirsky, Sonja. (2009). well-being and alleviating depressive symptoms with positive psychology interventions: A practice-friendly meta-analysis. Journal of clinical psychology. 65. 467–87.

33. What Is Depression? American Psychiatric Association. Retrieved 16 May 2020, from https://www.psychiatry.org/patients-families/depression/what-is-depression

34. Simmons, W. K., Burrows, K., Avery, J. A., Kerr, K. L., Bodurka, J., Savage, C. R., & Drevets, W. C. (2016). Depression-Related Increases and Decreases in Appetite: Dissociable Patterns of Aberrant Activity in Reward and Interoceptive Neurocircuitry. The American journal of psychiatry, 173(4), 418–428.

35. Pilgrim, A. L., Robinson, S. M., Sayer, A. A., & Roberts, H. C. (2015). An overview of appetite decline in older people. Nursing older people, 27(5), 29–35.

36. Berk, Lee & Prowse, Michelle & Bains, Gurinder & Batt, Jennifer & Petrofsky, Jerry & Daher, Noha & Danner, Harmony & Ludeman, Laura & Lahman, Michael & Tan, Stanley & Berk, Dottie. (2010). Humor-associated laughter affects appetite hormones. The FASEB Journal. 24.

37. Sleep Time Recommendations: What's Changed? SleepFounation.org Retrieved 16 May 2020, from https://www.sleepfoundation.org/articles/how-much-sleep-do-we-really-need

38. Cooke, J. R., & Ancoli-Israel, S. (2011). Normal and abnormal sleep in the elderly. Handbook of clinical neurology, 98, 653–665.

39. Doghramji K., (2019) Consequences of Poor Sleep in the Elderly MD Magazine. Retrieved 16 May 2020, from https://www.mdmag.com/insights/insomnia-elderly/consequences-of-poor-sleep-in-the-elderly

40. Kimata H. (2004). Reduction of plasma levels of neurotrophins by laughter in patients with atopic dermatitis. Pediatr Asthma Allergy Immunol. 17 (2):131–135.

41. Han, J.H., Park, K. M. & Park H. (2017). Effects of Laughter Therapy on Depression and Sleep among Patients at Long-term Care Hospitals. Korean Journal of Adult Nursing (Korean J Adult Nurs) Vol. 29 No. 5, 560–568.

42. Ko, H. & Youn, C. (2011). Effects of laughter therapy on depression, cognition and sleep among the community-dwelling elderly. Geriatrics & gerontology international. 11. 267–74.

43. Miller, M., & Fry, W. F. (2009). The effect of mirthful laughter on the human cardiovascular system. Medical hypotheses, 73(5), 636–639.

44. Breathe The Lung Association. On love, laughter and lungs (2017). Retrieved 17 May 2020, from https://www.lung.ca/blog/love-laughter-and-lungs

45. Little, A.C., Jones B.C, & DeBruine L.M. (2011). Facial attractiveness: evolutionary based research. Philos Trans R Soc Lond B Biol Sci.12; 366(1571): 1638–1659.

46. Popkin, B. M., D'Anci, K. E., & Rosenberg, I. H. (2010). Water, hydration, and health. Nutrition reviews, 68(8), 439–458.

47. British Nutrition Foundation, 2014 Dehydration in the elderly. Retrieved 18 May 2020, from https://www.nutrition.org.uk/nutritionscience/life/dehydrationelderly.html

48. Cowen, L. E., Hodak, S. P., & Verbalis, J. G. (2013). Age-associated abnormalities of water homeostasis. Endocrinology and metabolism clinics of North America, 42(2), 349–370.

49. Beck LH, Lavizzo-Mourey R. Geriatric hypernatremia [corrected] Ann Intern Med. 1987;107(5):768–769.

50. The Eatwell Guide. Retrieved 11 May 2020, from https://www.nhs.uk/live-well/eat-well/the-eatwell-guide/

51. Ramachandran, V.S. (2005) A Brief Tour of Human Consciousness: From Impostor Poodles to Purple Numbers. Pi Press; New Ed edition.

52. Lund, D. A., Utz, R., Caserta, M. S., & De Vries, B. (2008). Humor, laughter, and happiness in the daily lives of recently bereaved spouses. Omega, 58(2), 87–105.

53. Adamle, K. N., & Ludwick, R. (2005). Humor in hospice care: Who, where, and how much? American Journal of Hospice and Palliative Medicine, 22(4), 287–290.

54. Dean, R., & Gregory, D. (2004). Humor and laughter in palliative care: An ethnographic investigation. Palliative & supportive care. 2. 139–48.

55. Jackson D., Firtko, A., Edenborough, M. (2013). Personal resilience as a strategy for surviving and thriving in the face of workplace adversity: a literature review. Journal of Advanced Nursing, vol 60, no 1 pp 1–9.

56. How Do Humans Get Oxygen in Their Bodies? Retrieved 4 May 2020, from https://sciencing.com/humans-oxygen-bodies-10018091.html

57. Ma, X., Yue, Z. Q., Gong, Z. Q., Zhang, H., Duan, N. Y., Shi, Y. T., Wei, G. X., & Li, Y. F. (2017). The Effect of Diaphragmatic Breathing on Attention, Negative Affect and Stress in Healthy Adults. Frontiers in psychology, 8, 874.

58. Hymes, A., & Nuernberger, P. (1991). Breathing patterns found in heart attack patients. International Journal of Yoga Therapy, 2, 25–27.

PART TWO: SUPPORT

1. Anxiety UK, Anxiety UK Welcome New Social Anxiety Guidelines. Retrieved 4 April 2020, from https://www.anxietyuk.org.uk/anxiety-uk-welcome-new-social-anxiety-guidlines/
2. Socialanxietyinstitute.org. He Who Laughs Most is Most Likely to Last, Retrieved 8 April 2020, from https://socialanxietyinstitute.org/he-who-laughs-most
3. Zocdoc Answers, Medical questions & health advice by licensed doctors Retrieved 25 April 2020, from https://answers.zocdoc.com/details/4097/what-causes-one-to-cough-when-they-laugh
4. Parvizi, J., Anderson, S.W., Martin, C.0., Damasio, H., & Damasio, A.R.(2001) Pathological laughter and crying: A link to the cerebellum, Brain, Volume 124, Issue 9, Pages 1708–1719.
5. Vingerhoets, A., & Bylsma, L. M. (2016). The Riddle of Human Emotional Crying: A Challenge for Emotion Researchers. Emotion review: journal of the International Society for Research on Emotion, 8(3), 207–217.
6. Gračanin A, Bylsma LM, Vingerhoets A.J. (2014) Is crying a self-soothing behavior?. Front Psychol. 2014;5:502.
7. Platt, Tracey & Ruch, Willibald. (2009). The emotions of gelotophobes: Shameful, fearful, and joyless?. Humor-international Journal of Humor Research - HUMOR. 22. 91–110.
8. Scientific American. People with This Phobia Suffer from a Fear of Being Laughed at. Retrieved 25 April 2020, from https://www.scientificamerican.com/article/people-with-this-phobia-suffer-from-a-fear-of-being-laughed-at/
9. Ruch, Willibald & Proyer, René & Popa, D. (2008). The fear of being laughed at (gelotophobia) and personality.
10. Proyer, R., Ruch, W., Ali, N., Al-Olimat, H., Amemiya, T., Adal, T., Ansari, S., ...& Yeun, E. (2009). Breaking ground in cross-cultural research on the fear of being laughed at (gelotophobia): A multi-national study involving 73 countries Humor – International Journal of Humor Research, 22 (1–2).
11. Havranek, M. M., Volkart, F., Bolliger, B., Roos, S., Buschner, M., Mansour, R., Chmielewski, T., Gaudlitz, K., Hättenschwiler, J., Seifritz, E., & Ruch, W. (2017). The fear of being laughed at as additional diagnostic criterion in social anxiety disorder and avoidant personality disorder?. PloS one, 12(11), e0188024.
12. Ahmed, A., & Simmons, Z. (2013). Pseudobulbar affect: prevalence and management. Therapeutics and clinical risk management, 9, 483–489.
13. Multiple Sclerosis Trust. Inappropriate laughing or crying: how common is the pseudobulbar affect? Retrieved 25 April 2020, from https://www.mstrust.org.uk/latest/research-news/ms-research-update-inappropriate-laughing-or-crying-how-common-pseudobulbar
14. American Stroke Association. Pseudobulbar Affect (PBA). Retrieved 25 April 2020, from https://www.stroke.org/en/about-stroke/effects-of-stroke/emotional-effects-of-stroke/pseudobulbar-affect

RESEARCH, RESOURCES AND RECOMMENDED

Laughter, smiling and humour

Association for Applied and Therapeutic Humor: www.aath.org/
Bernstein M.J., Young, S.G., Brown C.M., Sacco D.F., and Claypool, H.M. (1998) Adaptive Responses to Social Exclusion Social Rejection Improves Detection of Real and Fake Smiles, Psychological Science, 19, 10, 981–983.

Bachorowski, J.A., & Owren, M.J. (2003). Reconsidering the evolution of nonlinguistic communication: The case of laughter. Journal of Nonverbal Behavior, 27, 183–199.

Bernstein M.J., Sacco D.F., Brown, C.M. Young, S.G. and Claypool, H.M. (2010) A preference for genuine smiles following social exclusion. Journal of Experimental Social Psychology, 46, 196–199.

Cohn, J.F., and Tronick E.Z. (1983) Three-Month-Old Infants' Reaction to Simulated Maternal Depression, Child Development, 54, 185–193.

Cousins, N. Radio Interview Transcription: Norman Cousins talks on Positive Emotions and Health (1983). Reprieved 19 January 2020 from: https://media.laughteryogaamerica.com/pdf/ncousins-interview.pdf

Darwin, C. (1872) The Expression of the Emotions in Man and Animals, London: J. Murray.

Duchenne G.B., (1990) The mechanism of human facial expression, trans. R.A. Cuthbertson, Cambridge University Press.

Ekman, P., Davidson, R.J., Friesen, W.V. (1990) The Duchenne Smile: Emotional Expression and Brain Physiology II, Journal of Personality and Social Psychology, 58, 342–353.

Ekman, P. Wallace V. Freisen, O'Sullivan M. (1988) Smiles when lying, Journal of Personality and Social Psychology, 54, 414–420.

Fredrickson, B.L., and Levenson, R.W. (1998) Positive emotions speed recovery from the cardiovascular sequelae of negative emotions, Cognition and Emotion, 12, 191–220.

Gray, A.W., Parkinson, B. & Dunbar, R.I. Laughter's Influence on the Intimacy of Self-Disclosure. Hum Nat 26, 28–43 (2015).

Harris, C.R. (1999). The mystery of ticklish laughter. American Scientist, 87, 344–351.

Hecht, M. A., & LaFrance, M. (1998). License or Obligation to Smile: The Effect of Power and Sex on Amount and Type of Smiling. Personality and Social Psychology Bulletin, 24(12), 1332–1342.

Hertenstein, M.J., Hansel, C.A., Butts A.M., Hile S.N. (2009) Smile intensity in photographs predicts divorce later in life. Motivation and Emotion. 33, 2, 99–105.

Holmes, J. Making Humour Work: Creativity on the Job, Applied Linguistics, Volume 28, Issue 4, December 2007, Pages 518–537.

Keltner D., and Bonanno, G (1997) A Study of Laughter and Dissociation: Distinct Correlates of Laughter and Smiling During Bereavement, Journal of Personality and Social Psychology, 73, 687–702.

Kimata, H. (2007). Laughter Elevates the Levels of Breast-Milk Melatonin. J Psychosom Res;62(6):699–702.
Kraft TL, Pressman SD. Grin and bear it: the influence of manipulated facial expression on the stress response. Psychol Sci. 2012;23(11):1372–1378.

Kraut, R.E., Johnston R.E. (1979) Social and Emotional Messages of Smiling: An Ethological Approach, Journal of Personality and Social Psychology, 37, 9, 1539–1553.

LaFrance M., Hecht, M.A., Paluck, E.L. (2003) The Contingent Smile: A Meta-Analysis of Sex Differences in Smiling, Psychological Bulletin, 129, 305–334.

Landis, C. (1924) Studies of Emotional Reactions II. General Behavior and Facial Expression, Journal of Comparative Psychology, 4, 5.
Livingstone, M.S. (2000) Is it warm? Is it real? Or just low spatial frequency? Science, 290, 1299.

Martin, J. D., Abercrombie, H. C., Gilboa-Schechtman, E., & Niedenthal, P. M. (2018). Functionally distinct smiles elicit different physiological responses in an evaluative context. Scientific reports, 8(1), 3558.

Mehua, M., Grammerb K., and Dunbara, R.I.M., (2007) Smiles when sharing, Evolution and Human Behavior, 28, 415–422.

Morreall, J. (1986) The Philosophy of Laughter and Humor, Publisher: SUNY Press.
Ozono H., et al. (2010) What's in a Smile? Cultural Differences in the Effects of Smiling on Judgments of Trustworthiness, Letters on Evolutionary Behavioral Science, 1, 15–18.

Platt, T., Ruch, W., & Proyer, R. (2009). A lifetime of fear of being laughed at Zeitschrift für Gerontologie und Geriatrie, 43 (1), 36-41.

Provine, R. (2000). Laughter: A scientific investigation. New York: Viking.
Provine, R. (2001) Laughter. Penguin.
Provine, R. (2004) Laughing, Tickling, and the Evolution of Speech and Self Current Directions in Psychological Science.13, (6) 215–218.
Ruch, W., Platt, T., Bruntsch, R., & Ďurka, R. (2017). Evaluation of a picture-based test for the assessment of gelotophobia. Frontiers in Psychology, 8, Article 2043.

Ruch, W., Platt T., Proyer R.T. & Chen H. (2019). Humor and Laughter, Playfulness and Cheerfulness: Upsides and Downsides to a Life of Lightness. Front. Psychol. 10.

Van Hooff, J. 1972, "A Comparative Approach to the Phylogeny of Laughter and Smiling," in Non-Verbal Communication, Robert A. Hinde (ed.), London: Cambridge University Press, pp. 209–241.

Vettin, J., & Todt, D. (2004). Laughter in conversation: Features of occurrence and acoustic structure. Journal of Nonverbal Behavior, 28(2), 93–115.

Yam, K.C., Christian, M.C., Wei, W., Liao, Z. & Nai, J.
The Mixed Blessing of Leader Sense of Humor: Examining Costs and Benefits
Academy of Management Journal 61 (1).

Yuki, M., Maddux, W.W., Masuda, T. (2007) Are the windows to the soul the same in the East and West? Cultural differences in using the eyes and mouth as cues to recognize emotions in Japan and the United States, Journal of Experimental Social Psychology, 43, 303–311.

Happiness and Well-being

Baumeister, R. F., Vohs, K. D., Nathan DeWall, C., & Zhang, L. (2007). How Emotion Shapes Behavior: Feedback, Anticipation, and Reflection, Rather Than Direct Causation. Personality and Social Psychology Review, 11(2), 167–203.
Brown, D. (2017) Happy: Why More or Less Everything is Absolutely Fine. Corgi.
Caste, A.D (2019) Better with Age: The Psychology of Successful Aging. Oxford University Press.

Cosco, Theodore & Prina, Matthew & Perales Puchalt, Jaime & Stephan, Blossom & Brayne, Carol. (2013). Operational definitions of successful aging: A systematic review. International psychogeriatrics / IPA. 26. 1–9.

Csikszentmihalyi', M. (2008). Flow: The Psychology of Optimal Experience Harper Perennial Modern Classics.

Eurich, T. (2017). The right way to be introspective (yes, there's a wrong way). TED. Retrieved 27 March 2020 from https://ideas.ted.com/the-right-way-to-be-introspective-yes-theres-a-wrong-way/

Fields in Trust, is a British charity that champions and supports parks and green spaces by protecting them for people to enjoy: http://www.fieldsintrust.org/

Fredrickson, B. L. (2009). Positivity. New York, NY: Crown.

Frey, W. (1985) Crying: The Mystery of Tears. Winston Pr.
Gable, S. L., & Haidt, J. (2005). What (and Why) is Positive Psychology? Review of General Psychology, 9(2), 103–110.

Gilbert, D. (2007). Stumbling on Happiness. Harper Perennial.

Glaze JE. (2001) Reflection as a transforming process: student advanced nurse practitioners' experiences of developing reflective skills as part of an MSc programme. J Adv Nurs. 34(5):639–647.

Harris, J. (2009) The Nurture Assumption: Why Children Turn Out the Way They Do Free Press.

Jans-Beken Phd, Lilian & Jacobs, Nele & Janssens, Mayke & Peeters, Sanne & Reijnders, Jennifer & Lechner, Lilian & Lataster, Johan. (2019). Gratitude and health: An updated review. The Journal of Positive Psychology. 1–40.

Johnson M. Embodied understanding. Front Psychol. 2015;6:875. Published 2015 June 29.

Kok, B. E., Coffey, K. A., Cohn, M. A., Catalino, L. I., Vacharkulksemsuk, T., Algoe, S. B., Fredrickson, B. L. (2013). How Positive Emotions Build Physical Health: Perceived Positive Social Connections Account for the Upward Spiral Between Positive Emotions and Vagal Tone. Psychological Science, 24(7), 1123–1132.

Lyubomirsky, S., Sheldon, K. M., & Schkade, D. (2005) : Pursuing happiness -The architecture of sustainable change. Review of General Psychology, 9, 111–131.

Medina, J. (2014) Brain Rules (Updated and Expanded): 12 Principles for Surviving and Thriving at Work, Home, and School. Pear Press; Second edition.
Pennebaker, J. W. (1997). Writing About Emotional Experiences as a Therapeutic Process. Psychological Science, 8(3), 162–166.

Pfaff, D.W. (2015) The Altruistic Brain: How We Are Naturally Good. 1st Edition. Oxford University Press.

Ramachandran, V (2009). TEDIndia. The neurons that shaped civilization. Retrieved 18 February 2020 from: https://www.ted.com/talks/vilayanur_ramachandran_the_neurons_that_shaped_civilization?language=en

Roos V., Zaaiman R. (2017) Active Ageing as Positive Intervention: Some Unintended Consequences. In: Proctor C. (eds) Positive Psychology Interventions in Practice. Springer, Cham.

Seneca, (2005) On the Shortness of Life: Life Is Long If You Know How to Use It (Penguin Great Ideas). Penguin Books.
Scientific American. (2011) A Brief Guide to Embodied Cognition: Why You Are Not Your Brain Retrieved 18 March 2020 from:
https://blogs.scientificamerican.com/guest-blog/a-brief-guide-to-embodied-cognition-why-you-are-not-your-brain/

Shames, L (1990), Not Fade Away: A Short Life Well Lived. Harper Perennial.

Steindl-Rast, D TEDTALK (2013): Want to be happy? Be grateful:https://www.ted.com/talks/david_steindl_rast_want_to_be_happy_be_grateful
Wellenzohn, S., Proyer, R.T., & Ruch, W. (2016). Humor-based online positive psychology interventions: A randomized placebo-controlled long-term trial. Journal of Positive Psychology, 11(6), 584–594.
Wood, K. (2013). The Lost Art of Introspection: Why You Must Master Yourself. Expert Enough. Retrieved from http://expertenough.com/2990/the-lost-art-of-introspection-why-you-must-master-yourself

Zander, R., & Zander, B.(2000). The Art of Possibility: Transforming Professional and Personal Life. Harvard Business Review Press.

Printed in Great Britain
by Amazon

43979993R00116